Doctrine and Poetry

Augustine's Influence on Old English Poetry

BERNARD F. HUPPÉ

*Professor of English, Harpur College
of the State University of New York*

STATE UNIVERSITY OF NEW YORK

1959

Library of Congress Catalog Card Number: 59-7529

Manufactured in the United States of America
by the Quinn & Boden Company, Inc., Rahway, N. J.

In affection
this book is dedicated
to my sisters

Preface

Saint Augustine formulates a Christian theory of literature in the *De doctrina Christiana,* a work which provides, according to H.-I. Marrou, the basic program for a Christian culture. This program found widespread approval in early medieval theory—so this book will argue—and had positive influence upon the early practice of poetry in the vernacular, specifically Old English.

This study begins with an exposition of the Augustinian literary theory as it is formulated in the *De doctrina.* The continuing influence of the theory will be shown by reference to the indispensable Isidore of Seville, as well as the obscure rhetorician, Vergil of Toulouse; by reference in particular to Bede and his continental successors, Alcuin and Rabanus, but also to Scotus Erigena. The study of the practice of Christian poetry in the Old English vernacular will be preceded by a glance at Christian poetry in Latin for what light it sheds on the vernacular practice. The influence of Augustinian theory on vernacular practice will be illustrated in detailed analysis of several brief poems and of one very long poem, *Genesis A.* Finally, some concluding remarks will be made

v

Preface

on the implications of the theory for a systematic study of the body of Old English poetry.

The basic work on this book was completed in Princeton, New Jersey, in 1950; in awaiting publication it has been revised and twice rewritten. During a Fulbright year (1955-1956) in Austria, I had the opportunity to examine pertinent exegetical materials in very early manuscripts at Vienna and at Admont. It was a pleasure for which I am most grateful. The present publication has been made possible through a grant of the Research Foundation of the State University of New York. I wish to express my thanks for their helpfulness to Mort Grant, Secretary of the Foundation, and to Professor Chandler Brooks, Chairman of the Publications Committee of the University's Graduate Council.

To my two good friends, John Weld of Harpur and D. W. Robertson, Jr., of Princeton, I owe more than mere thanks can repay. I wish the book might be as wise and good as their counsels deserve.

To Mary Lois Huppé go my loving thanks.

Bernard F. Huppé

August 1, 1958

Contents

Doctrine and Poetry

Chapter I

POETIC THEORY IN THE
DE DOCTRINA CHRISTIANA

PLATO cabined and confined the poet to the point
of excluding him from the Republic. Augustine in his
De doctrina Christiana seems to leave the poet, if it were
possible, even less room. "A man speaks more or less
wisely," he says, "in so far as he is more or less proficient
in Holy Scriptures." [1] The proportion is mathematical
and apparently leaves no freedom for the imagination.
The avowed purpose of the *De doctrina* is to give in-
struction, not in letters, but in the study and exposition
of the Bible, for Scripture contains the whole sum of
wisdom: "Whatever outside of Scripture a man learns,
if evil is condemned, if useful is found in Scripture." [2]
Further, Scripture contains "matters which cannot be
found except in its wonderful sublimity and simplicity."
Understanding of the Bible is the end of all serious study,
and the Bible itself is the model and guide for all serious

3

writing; secular learning is as nothing compared with spiritual learning.[3]

Yet Augustine does not simply reject poetry; he maintains for it an important, if subsidiary, place in his scheme of culture. The proper relation between Scripture and secular letters is established by Augustine in the *De doctrina* by reference to an allegorical interpretation of the Old Testament story of the departure of the Israelites from Egypt. According to this account the Israelites, when they departed from Egypt, took with them a small treasure of silver and gold but left behind pagan idols. In this, St. Augustine, following exegetical tradition, saw more than mere history. The idols and the treasure symbolize two aspects of "human learning": the idols symbolize "lying and superstitious fictions, which the Christian ought to avoid and abominate"; the gold and silver taken by the Israelites symbolize "whatever human learning is useful and is gathered in pagan books." [4] The actions of the Israelites, thus interpreted, inculcate a lesson in the proper handling of pagan and human learning: the Christian should not ignore such learning but should use what of it is valuable for his purposes, discarding what is false. At the same time the Christian must be guided by his awareness that human learning is merely ancillary to scriptural learning, for, as Augustine proceeds with his interpretation, the treasure taken out of Egypt, i.e., human learning, was as nothing compared to the treasure amassed in Jerusalem by the time of Solomon, this treasure symbolizing, "the knowledge gained from Scripture." Human learning is thus but a bare beginning for the Christian, a humble servant to scriptural learning.

However limiting, Augustine's attitude toward pagan culture is quite humane. To be sure, in his *Confessions* he exercises his unsentimental wit at the expense of his youthful, bathetic reading of Dido's death, and in the fourth book of the *De doctrina* he rather contemptuously disavows any intention of writing a secular rhetoric: Augustine, bound on his single-minded journey, is willing, if need be, to stop his ears completely to the literature he had "learned and taught in the public schools," [5] but he is equally prepared to listen to any poem that proves useful for his journey. Believing that the highest aim of the Christian writer is to explain the Bible, Augustine is not driven by zeal to an outright condemnation of secular letters. To say that the study of eloquence is subsidiary to the reading and expounding of Scripture is not to deny its importance for civilized and educated man: "Let us learn without pride whatever may be learned from man." [6] The question for Augustine is not a simple choice between the good and the bad. The Bible is fundamental, not exclusive, not the denial but the model of all that is highly serious in human writing. Not only in his interpretation of the Flight from Egypt, but elsewhere in the *De doctrina*, Augustine strongly defends the study of pagan letters where they are of value for understanding Scripture. "We ought not," he says, "to cease to learn letters because pagans asserted Mercury to be their discoverer. . . . Indeed anyone who is a good, true Christian, wherever he discovers the truth,

5

will know that it belongs to his Master." [7] The rules of true eloquence are divinely ordained and "are none the less true although they may be used to persuade of the false; but because they can also be used to persuade of the good, the faculty itself is not guilty, but the evil perversity of the one misusing it." [8]

This distinction between an object and the use to which the object is put is central to the argument of the *De doctrina,* which begins, in fact, with Augustine's brilliant distinction between the *use* and the *enjoyment* of an object. By means of this distinction he attempts to reconcile the idea of God with the fact of evil. He begins with two assumptions: that God is good and that God created all things. Since created objects cannot be in themselves evil, evil pertains only to the use and enjoyment of the objects of creation, not to the objects themselves. The end of man is happiness; the objects of creation, which are neutral, cannot themselves give happiness since God is the only source of joy. It follows that the objects of creation cannot be *enjoyed* for themselves but that they can be *used* toward the end of enjoying God. Such use of the objects of creation is alone proper, so that to use them for any other end than the enjoyment of God is not *use* but *abuse.* To attempt to enjoy what may only be *used* is to be involved in contradiction; and to believe that one may *enjoy* any earthly object for itself is folly. Augustine concludes with a memorable picture of the pilgrimage of man's life inexorably ruled by the consequences of choice between the true use and false use (abuse) of earthly goods:

To *enjoy* is to cling in love to something for itself. To *use*, however, is to relate what is used to obtaining what you love, provided that ought to be loved. (For wrongful use should properly be called wasting or abuse.) Wherefore, if we are pilgrims who cannot live happily except in our native land, if desiring in this pilgrimage to use our wretched goods and to end our wretchedness, we wish to return to the native land, it is necessary that we be able to attain to the native land, *which is to be enjoyed,* by means of the vehicles of land and sea, *which are to be used;* but if the sweetness of the journey and the very pleasure in the vehicles should delight us, so that diverted to enjoying those things which we ought to use, we do not desire hastily to finish the journey, involved in perverse temptation, we lose our citizenship in the native land, the delight of which should make us blessed: thus in the life of this mortality, being pilgrims from the Lord, if we wish to return to the native land, where we may be blessed, *we must use this world, we must not enjoy it.*[9]

From Augustine's doctrine of use it follows that what is wrong with eloquence is not the practice of eloquence but making the practice an end in itself, *clinging to it in love,* in disregard of the example set by the sacred writers, like Paul, "who possess, but do not make a display of eloquence." [10] Pagan writers, on the contrary, constantly revealed their folly in making a display of eloquence. They valued eloquence for its own sake. How concerned Augustine was to make the principle clear, how important it was to him to inculcate a proper attitude toward letters is shown in his *De catechizandis rudibus,* which treats of methods for instructing beginners in the Faith. Catechumens who have had training in pagan eloquence, Augustine warns, should be taught to look back on their learning in the light of Christian truth "lest they presume to compare with the pure heart, the trained tongue which formerly they preferred." They must be specially taught, he continues, "to heed Holy Scripture so that solid eloquence will not distress them because it is uninflated." [11]

The contrast between the "solid eloquence" of Scripture and the "inflated" eloquence of the pagan writers is at the heart of Augustine's aesthetic theory. The reason why newly made Christians, trained in pagan eloquence, found the eloquence of Scripture disappointing was that this eloquence is "solid" (*solidum*). When Augustine calls scriptural eloquence "solid," he implies a primary contrast between it and pagan eloquence. The former is solid because it is concerned with revealed meaning (light); such eloquence is to be judged on its power to convey spiritual truth with moving conviction. Pagan eloquence is "inflated," i.e. empty, because in the absence of Christian revelation it is concerned merely with manner of expression (sweetness); such eloquence is to be judged merely for its skill with the outward forms of language (letter). Thus, in order to appreciate the Bible persons of pagan learning had to make an important change in their habits of reading and thinking. They had to learn "that meanings (*sententiae*) are more important than words, just as the spirit is superior to the body." Specifically, the pagan-trained catechumen had learned to concentrate on the "fleshly robes" (the letter) of literature. In contrast when he read the Bible he had to avoid reading "according to the letter," the "fleshly robes" in which Scripture is "wrapped up and concealed." These robes of the literal existed only "to be unwrapped

and made open for the sake of underlying meaning."
Only in the unraveling of an allegory could readers be
stirred by biblical truths.[12]

Charm of style is, at its best, of accessory importance,
since it cannot in itself bring to the mind of man the con-
viction of divine truth; moreover, charm of style pursued
for its own sake is most dangerous. "For the sake of charm
an enormous amount of trouble has been expended by
men," and, careless of the truth, they have urged wicked-
ness elegantly, caring only, Augustine says, "that they
may be read avidly for pleasure alone." [13] This distinc-
tion helps us to understand the place of aesthetic pleasure
in Augustine's poetics. Because the eloquence of the
Bible is a mirror in human language of the eloquence of
God, the Bible is the supreme model for all true elo-
quence. But the eloquence of Scripture is pre-eminently
due to the profundity of its revealed truth, its light; the
sweetness of its rhetorical pattern derives from revela-
tion; rhetoric is not something separate, to be learned
without reference to divine truth.

The aesthetic pleasure which accompanies true read-
ing of Christian literature for Augustine is not directly
related to the perception of the forms and patterns of the
rhetoricians, but rather to the discovery of underlying
truth. Specifically, the Bible was "divinely ordained" to
be obscure, in order to prevent slackening of attention
when the intellect was not strenuously engaged. As
Marrou has shown, exercise, *gymnastique intellectuelle*,
is, for Augustine, an essential part of the process of the
mind moving toward divine truth.[14] Only when the

9

muscles of the mind have become supple, have been prepared for accomplishment far beyond the ordinary, can man realize the beauty of revealed truth. The difficulties of the Bible serve to keep the unprepared from trying to grasp what they cannot understand, but more than this they are necessary if the mind is to perceive the beautiful. In literature a relation exists between difficulty and pleasure, for, as Augustine points out, a truth, simply and directly presented, may have no effect on the mind; whereas the same truth, concealed in a difficult allegorical presentation, may move the mind through pleasure:

> How is it, I ask, that if anyone says there are men of perfect sanctity through whose lives and manners the Church of Christ redeems those who come to it, . . . he delights the hearer less than if he had expounded that part of the Song of Songs where, with the same underlying meaning, it is said of the Church, praised as a beautiful woman: *Thy teeth are like a flock of sheep that are shorn, which come up from the washing, whereof every one bears twins and none is barren among them.* Does a man actually learn anything more than when he hears the same thing in the plainest words, without the aid of this figure of speech? And yet, I know not why, I contemplate the saints more pleasingly when I see them as the teeth of the Church tearing men from errors. . . . No one has any doubt that some things are understood more readily through figures of speech, and that when something is searched for with difficulty, it is, as a result, more delightfully discovered.[15]

The interpretation imposed by the obscurity of the language provides a specific literary pleasure. Obscurity, allegory, symbol are pleasurable means of revealing

Christian beauty. "The more they seem to be obscure through their use of figurative expressions," Augustine says of the Prophets, "the more they give pleasure when they have been made clear." [16] Thus, the Christian need not relinquish the literary pleasures cherished by the pagan; he may find instead a similar but truer pleasure in discovering through the difficulties of allegory an underlying meaning which lifts the mind toward God. This pleasure is a real pleasure, though not of the sensibilities but of the mind.[17]

The importance given by Augustine to the factor of obscurity in writing seems, however, to contradict his frequent insistence on the need for clarity and simplicity in writing. Actually, no contradiction is involved. He does not warn the learned catechumen against rhetoric, as such; rather he warns him of his exclusive delight in it. What he attacks is not meaningful obscurity but meaningless rhetorical display. The rhetoric of the Second Sophistic might well have dismayed him, not because it taught obscurity, but because it treated obscurity as an end in itself. He addresses himself less against the use of figures, as Marrou points out, than against "esoteric expressions, unusual and over-refined terms, difficult constructions, in one word, the amphigoric style with pretensions to learning." [18] It is not the use of symbol and allegory that Augustine deplores, but rhetoric for the sake of rhetoric. As Marrou further points out, Augustine "says in the *Confessions* that he prefers the fables of the poets to the errors of the philosophers because the former (the allusion to allegories is obvious) could be led to be a true nourishment for the soul." At Cassiacum, Augustine even defended poetry against "the contempt of his young disciples" and advised "Licentius to complete his interrupted poem on Pyramus and Thisbe in celebrating under their name the pure love in which the soul is united to the understanding by means of philosophy." [19]

To be sure, in Book IV of the *De doctrina* he seems unequivocally to reject all but the simplest writing: "We are not to think that the sacred writers are to be imitated by us in those places where . . . they speak with useful and healthy obscurity." But the context of the statement serves to limit the applicability of the rejection. Augustine specifically addresses "the interpreters of the sacred writers." Since they are explaining what is obscure and difficult, they ought themselves to "labor primarily to be understood." [20] Augustine, by his own insistence, is not writing a book of rhetoric suitable to the uses of Christian poets. The distinction involved is simply the distinction between writing a poem and explaining one. It would not be incumbent on the poet to aim at the clarity of the biblical exegete; rather he would attempt, as he was able, to follow the practice of the sacred writers. Instruction in such writing Augustine left to others, "competent men willing in the spirit of benevolence to undertake the labor for the advantage of their brethren." [21] Augustine did not himself have the time. Moreover, St. Augustine, when he wrote Book IV of the *De doctrina*, had little need any longer for the aid of the poetry; one must suppose that he felt it to be a waste of valuable time for the proficient Christian. At the same time Augustine was keenly alive to the needs of the ordinary Christian. He was far from despising the means necessary to encourage the Faith among the people. Secular Christian literature finds no proponent in Augustine; on the other hand, it finds in him no opponent. Indeed, by implication, his theory clearly points the way toward the serious literature of the Middle Ages.

The Christian poet, though he would not have found in the *De doctrina* any specific practical assistance, would have found in it clear theoretical expression of what he should attempt and what he should avoid, as, for example, in Augustine's discussion of certain verses in which Claudian suggests that Neptune can be taken seriously as a symbol. On Claudian's poetic rationalization Augustine pours contempt, not because it is wrong to write poetry, not because his poetry is bad, but precisely because the verse is melodious—and wrongheadedly empty. He says, "This husk shakes noisy pebbles within its sweet cover; but it provides food for pigs, not men; he knows what I mean who knows the Gospel." The shell—what he elsewhere calls the "fleshly robes"—is attractive, but the source of the beautiful, the truth within, is meaningless, a pebble which rattles and makes no sense. Augustine's figure of the shell and the kernel reveals most clearly his conception of the relations between the literal level and the level of meaning, *sententia*.[22] The kernel is what is important; it is to get at this that we crack the shell. The shell has no other value. Eloquence unrelated to the revelation of truth is a hollow shell. The perception

13

of the truly beautiful comes not from the shell, but from gaining to the kernel after the labor of breaking the shell.

But beyond establishing in a basic figure the relation between letter and sentence (underlying meaning), Augustine in his discussion of the verse subtly exemplifies the method by which the Christian should discover the underlying meaning in the figurative. Augustine says, quite simply, that he will be understood by one "who knows the Gospel." The hint should be sufficient. Indeed, it should be most easy to discover what Augustine means since the word "husks" (*siliqua*) is found in the Bible only in Luke 15:16, in the Parable of the Prodigal Son: "And he would fain have filled his belly with the husks that the swine did eat." Except for the use of the word "husks," however, the parable seems to cast little light on Augustine's meaning. The point is that Augustine was not thinking of the letter of the parable but of the symbolic meaning of the word "husks" as it is used in the parable. To know this meaning is to know the Bible in Augustine's way of thinking. Merely being able to spot the verbal parallel shows in itself only familiarity with the Bible, not knowledge of it.[23]

To know the Bible is to know that "the husks with which the Prodigal Son fed the pigs represent the pagan teachings, rattling in sterile vanity." Claudian's verses had to do, we recall, with a justification of Neptune on symbolic grounds; similarly, the husks, the pagan teachings, "in varied speech and song rang with the praises of the idols and of the fables about the pagan gods—in which the devils delighted." To go to Claudian's verses in search of spiritual sustenance would be to find oneself like the Prodigal Son, who, "when he wished to fill himself with the husks, wished, that is, to find in pagan teachings something solid and true which pertained to the happy life, but could not." The explanation just given is not, of course, to be found in the *De doctrina;* Augustine feels it necessary merely to give the hint: "He who knows the Gospel will know what I mean." But the words are Augustine's and appear in his exegetical treatise, *Quaestiones evangeliorum.*[24]

But Augustine would not yet have been content with a knowledge of Scripture that went only this far and did not call to mind another relevant passage in the Bible. Knowledge of the Bible, for Augustine, implied the ability to connect and relate various passages of Scripture. The stones in the husks which are food for swine should bring to mind the pearls of Matthew 7:6, which are *not* to be cast before swine. These pearls signify for Augustine the opposite of what the husks signify; they represent "whatever spiritual things are to be greatly admired; and because they lie in concealment and are sometimes brought up from the depths, these spiritual things, as if hidden in shells, are found in the covering of allegory." [25] In the figure of the pearls that are not to be, like the stone-filled husks, thrown to the swine, true Christian allegory is represented positively. Claudian's verses, no matter how exquisitely handled, no matter how beautiful in their imagery, are not beautiful, because, in singing the praises of Neptune, they merely rattle lies. They do not have the beauty of the pearls of truth.

Doctrine and Poetry

In his brief attack on the verses of Claudian, Augustine gives authoritative utterance to the figure of the shell and the kernel, which becomes in medieval usage almost a technique for distinguishing in importance between the levels of letter and sentence (underlying meaning); in addition he distinguishes clearly and sharply between false and true eloquence, thus aiding the poet to follow the right way by avoiding what Augustine castigates in Claudian; also he illustrates, through the leading suggestion of a masterful teacher, the basic method of ascertaining the truly beautiful in poetry. Finally, in his illustration he reveals that the beauty of poetry rests in an absolutely functional relationship between external form and inner meaning. The external form should bristle with a challenge to find an inner meaning; it is a shell to be cracked for the rich kernel. The "aesthetic moment" comes when the shell has been with difficulty opened to reveal the contents. Claudian's verses are lacking in true beauty, Augustine feels, because, although the shell is pretty, when it is opened one finds that the pretty sound produced is made by meaningless stones.

In contrast, the Christian poet will, like Augustine himself in his sermons, write pleasingly in such a way as to attract the hearer. The Christian poet will encourage the hearer, through intellectual exercise, to aspire to the understanding of divine truth. But he will, of course, be careful not to write eloquently for the sake of eloquence, to embellish for the sake of the beauty of the "fleshly robe," because style is not pleasing for its own sake. "That charm is not delightful," Augustine says, "in which although falsehoods are not spoken, unimportant and fragile truths are ornamented with a foamy copiousness of words." [26] Pleasure in the charm of style often leads, Augustine warns, to carelessness about truth and even to the promotion of wickedness. This literary pleasure, divorced from truth, is the basis for the popularity of the fables and fictions, which, as such, have no part in Christian literature, for true aesthetic pleasure derives from the understanding of God's truth (use). False pleasures, as in lying songs, come from man's own corrupted nature, from his turning away from God (abuse). [27]

But fables are not in themselves reprehensible. Although they are "devised for the pleasure of souls whose food is trifles," they may be used quite properly for instruction, as for example, by the grammarian. [28] A fable may be made to serve Christian truth; it ceases then to be a lying fable. That is why Augustine urged Licentius to continue with his Pyramus and Thisbe, which would celebrate an aspect of Christian charity. The fabulous and the fictitious enjoyed without reference to divine truth were anathema, but used for a purpose consonant with truth, fables might be employed, since the Christian would employ "without pride whatever may be learned from man." Used for an evil purpose the Bible itself, in certain passages, might seem to give comfort to sinners—to bigamists, for example. But against such misuse of the Bible, Augustine points out, St. Paul inveighed when he said: "The letter kills, but the spirit vivifies" (II Cor. 3:6).

17

The principle enunciated by St. Paul is fundamental to the Christian theory of literature. It was taken in general terms as teaching the need "to penetrate, by means of the vivifying spirit, to the inside of spiritual words." [29] Augustine applies this general principle specifically to the method of interpreting "the ambiguities of figurative speech." For in reading what is obscure and difficult "it is from the start necessary to avoid taking the figurative as literal." [30] A method of reading the Bible—or any work of serious Christian inspiration—follows from Augustine's application of the precept that the letter kills. The first effort of the reader must be to ascertain whether what he reads is literal or figurative. To mistake here is to fall into serious error, so that Augustine is constrained to set forth at length "the method of discovering whether a locution is literal or figurative." Underlying the method is the principle that the Bible and works modeled on the Bible are governed by the object of promoting charity, the love of God. As Augustine established at the beginning of the *De doctrina,* the purpose of man is to love God. God alone is to be enjoyed, and all else is to be used to this end. The purpose of literature is the promotion of charity to the end that God may be enjoyed. "Charity" Augustine defines as "the motion of the spirit toward loving God for His own sake and one's neighbor because of God." The opposite of charity is "cupidity, the motion of the spirit toward enjoying oneself, one's neighbor, and any bodily thing not because of God." "Scripture," Augustine says, "teaches nothing except charity and condemns nothing but cupidity." From this concept of Scripture follows a method of discovering whether a passage therein is literal or figurative: "in all cases this is the method: whatever in Scripture cannot literally be related to purity of life or to the truth of faith, may be taken as figurative." Augustine defines what he means by "purity of life" and "truth of faith": the former "pertains to *loving* God and your neighbor," the other "to understanding God and your neighbor." [31] They are, that is, aspects of charity. A Christian work of literature, therefore, must be written in order to promote charity. In turn the reader must be prepared to ponder what he hears or reads; he is directly enjoined by Augustine to search for the underlying meaning where the surface meaning does not satisfy the demands of true doctrine: "In regard to figurative passages, a rule like the following shall be observed: *what is read must be diligently turned over in the mind until an interpretation is found that promotes the reign of charity.*" [32]

The conception of poetry thus inculcated must have been very different from our own. As Marrou points out: "Between this symbolism and ours the distance is great because there the image is made to serve the reason and not, as with us, the sensibilities; the symbol is not intended to express a kind of revelation *sui generis* which escapes the discursive reason, but quite simply to veil a perfectly definite truth, easy to formulate in clear language." [33] De Labriolle makes much the same point about the allegorical process. He points out that we do not know the Bible as Christians of earlier centuries did, so that we miss the force of many biblical citations; the very process "of relating to the scriptural text, cost what may, all the thoughts which life can suggest in its infinite variety of vicissitudes may seem to us like a paradoxical wager which appears to succeed only through the subtlety of the commentator. We seem not so much to wonder at *tours de force* like these as to be disconcerted by them." [34] Augustine's statement, for example, that he takes great delight in thinking of the saints as the teeth of the Church is disconcerting. But we cannot begin to understand how Augustine read allegory until we are prepared to examine the program of training which made such reading possible.

The program as it is outlined in Books II and III of the *De doctrina* begins with the admonition that the student approach his work in the fear of the Lord, in humility. Only with such an attitude, and with the clear purpose before him of achieving charity, could the student avoid the temptation, which the study of letters placed in his path, to love the letter and not the underlying meaning that the letter served. The student's first concrete task after his spiritual preparation was to learn the Bible, by heart, word for word, or at least, so that it was completely familiar to him. In this way he could explain some obscurities in Scripture simply by reference to other passages which were clear. From the outset the Augustinian training was designed to make the competent reader keep the various portions of Scripture in mind so that he could with ease refer from one part to another. Next the student was to learn languages as an important aid to his understanding of the literal. He was to become acquainted with natural history because of the frequent figurative reference in the Bible to the habits of animals or to the properties of stones and plants. This scientific knowledge was to be purely utilitarian; that is, its purpose was to make clear the meaning of figurative references in the Bible. It was an applied science. To the same end study of numbers was to be pursued. Numbers have a very basic symbolic import; their use in the Bible is always meaningful. Music was to be studied for the same reason; principles of harmonic relation are helpful in understanding the Bible. The student was to learn musical theory, not practice. In general Augustine advises acquaintance with the sciences of the pagans while carefully putting to one side their "superstitions" and distinguishing between what is useful and what is useless for a specifically Christian culture centering in the study of the Bible.

History is an especially useful study, not only because it aids in fixing events chronologically in Scripture, but chiefly "because things that have happened and cannot be done again are to be considered as belonging to the course of time, the Author and Administrator of which is God." [35] Human history, like natural history, is worth studying, because the history of the world is in itself a symbolic book written by God and to be understood through the Bible. This concept of history is important because it includes the possibility of extending the limits of the method of biblical exegesis to include all creation and all experiences. In considering the medieval literature that is influenced by Augustinian exegetical theory it is necessary to bear in mind the Augustinian view of the symbolism in historical and natural events as well as in the Bible.

This résumé is not intended to establish in detail Augustine's actual program of study, for Augustine himself is more concerned with theory than with details of practice. An obvious relationship could be shown between Augustine's program and the classical and medieval discipline of the liberal arts, but the important point here is to show how completely Augustine bends all study toward the one goal of reading the Bible for its underlying meaning.[36] The student is never allowed to forget that everything in literature and in life is symbolic, is meaningful. His mind is exercised constantly so that it will be prepared to understand the word of God and His creation, whatever the obscurity and difficulty of their literal or outward forms. The end of learning is constantly stressed: no subject is to be studied for its own sake but only as it aids in a better understanding of God's truth. The system is almost the reverse of our own.

The import of the program and its consequent effect on the attitude of Christians toward reading is made even clearer in Book III of the *De doctrina*. The program has up to this point dealt with studies preparatory to a consideration of figurative obscurity, studies which will enable the student to solve obvious scriptural difficulties. The same information is necessary in understanding figurative ambiguities, but further instruction is also needed. A good knowledge of grammar is presupposed. The student must be prepared to resolve difficulties that are merely of the letter by a close attention to such matters as the punctuation of his text. With such knowledge he is prepared in the manner previously sketched to distinguish between the literal and the figurative on the basis of whether the literal is in accord with dogma. Guided by the principle that the figurative expression must be "turned in every way until the true underlying meaning (*sententiam veritatis*) is arrived at," [37] the student may now turn to a study of the rules governing figurative language. He will learn that figurative words have one meaning in one context but may have a different, even an opposite, meaning in another context. A symbol, depending on context, may represent either good or evil. [38] The purpose of turning over a figurative expression involves not only a close reading for context of the passage being studied but also a summoning up of other relevant passages in the Bible for what light they may cast on the meaning of the figure. It also involves a knowledge of the tropes and figures of rhetoric. Knowledge of the mechanics of the trope or figure often aids in unraveling the difficulties of the figurative. [39]

Here, in brief, is Augustine's theory of literature. Its basic premise is that the Bible, as the word of God, is not only the worthiest subject for man's intellectual efforts but also the model of all that is best in human discourse. Since it would be manifestly absurd to read the word of God for the letter rather than for meaning, the Bible (and serious literature in general) was not to be read "for the story," or for "charm of style," which afford false and deceiving pleasures in that they imply an attempt to enjoy an object of creation for itself. Thus we learn from the model to look first in all that we read at what is said. A straightforward exposition of dogma need be read simply with care and attention, but figurative writing, which is obscure or ambiguous through reason of fable or image, must be "turned over in the mind until an interpretation is found which promotes the reign of charity." The process of "turning over in the mind" is illustrated in Augustine's interpretation of a verse from the Song of Songs and, indirectly, in his demonstration of the emptiness of Claudian's verses. Aesthetic pleasure derives, according to Augustine, from the very discovery of hidden meanings; the quality of the pleasure has a direct relation to the difficulty of the ambiguities to be resolved. As the mind is exercised it is prepared to receive with warmth and delight the dogmatic truth which stated plainly might be accompanied by no pleasurable movement of the mind.

Here is the theory, but what of its influence? Does the theory provide guidance in the interpretation of early medieval poetry? To answer these questions it is necessary to glance briefly at the development of the Christian theory of literature as it is expounded by some representative writers of the early Middle Ages.

NOTES TO CHAPTER I

1. *De doctrina Christiana*, 4, 7(5). All translations are original, unless otherwise noted.
2. *Ibid.*, Prologue. See H.-I. Marrou, *Saint Augustin et la fin de la culture antique* (Paris, 1938), p. 376.
3. *De doctrina*, 2, 63(42).
4. *Ibid.*, 60(40).
5. *Ibid.*, 4, 1(2).
6. *Ibid.*, Prologue, 5.
7. *Ibid.*, 2, 28(18).
8. *Ibid.*, 54(36).
9. *Ibid.*, 1, 4(4).
10. *Ibid.*, 4, 14(7).
11. *De catechizandis rudibus*, 13(9).
12. *Ibid.*, 13(9). See E. K. Rand, *Founders of the Middle Ages* (2d ed.; Cambridge, 1941), pp. 1-68, 268-269; Marrou, *op. cit.*, pp. 392-396.
13. *De doctrina*, 4, 14(30).
14. Marrou, *op. cit.*, p. 308; see also the ensuing discussion, pp. 308-321, and p. 486: "Le prix de ce travail exégètique est donc indépendant de la découverte qu'il permet de faire; c'est le travail lui-même que les difficultés du texte exigent de l'esprit qui intérresse ici Augustin, il a une valeur propre." See also the supplementary "Retractatio" (Paris, 1949), pp. 646-651.
15. *De doctrina*, 2, 7-8(6).
16. *Ibid.*, 4, 15(7).
17. Marrou, *op. cit.*, pp. 490-491: "Ainsi le travail que nous impose la présence des obscurités de l'Ecriture apparaît en dernière analyse comme relevant moins de l'ordre purement religieux que de celui des valeurs humaines, de l'ordre de la culture. . . . Voici que l'exégèse allégorique réintroduit avec la poésie une activité qu'il faut bien appeler littéraire, artistique." See P. de Labriolle, *Histoire de la littérature latin chrétienne*, revised, G. Bardy (Paris, 1947), pp. 11-13.
18. Marrou, *op. cit.*, p. 535. See *De doctrina*, 4, 31(14).
19. Marrou, *op. cit.*, p. 497.

25

20. *De doctrina,* 4, 22(9).
21. *Ibid.,* 2, 59(39).
22. *Ibid.,* 3, 11(7). The verses were formerly attributed to Claudian, but are no longer considered to be by him. For an early statement of the distinction between letter and sentence see Eucherius of Lyons, *Formularum spiritalis intelligentiae, PL,* 50, 728: "Corpus ergo Scripturae sacrae, sicut traditur, in littera sive historia: est anima in morali sensu, qui tropicus dicitur: spiritus in superiore intellectu, qui anagoge apellatur. Quam triplicem Scriptuarum regulam convenienter observat confessio sanctae Trinitatis, sanctificans nos per omnia, ut integer spiritus noster, et anima et corpus sine querela in adventum Domini nostri Jesu Christi judiciumque servetur (I Thess. 5:23)." For information about Eucherius see U. Moricca, *Storia della letteratura latina cristiana* (Turin, 1932), III, pp. 851-858. On the general problem of letter and sentence, see C. Spicq, *Esquisse d'une histoire de l'exégèse latine* (Paris, 1944), p. 19; B. Smalley, *The Study of the Bible in the Middle Ages* (2d ed.; New York, 1952), pp. 1-25. (The present book was completed before the revised second edition appeared.)
23. See *De doctrina,* 4, 7(5).
24. *Quaestiones evangeliorum,* 2, 33.
25. *De sermone in monte,* 2, 68(20).
26. *De doctrina,* 4, 31(14).
27. *Ibid.,* 2, 39(25).
28. *De catechizandis rudibus,* 10(6).
29. Eucherius, *op. cit., PL,* 50, 727: "Nam cum littera occidat, spiritus autem vivificet (II Cor. 3:6), necesse est ad illa spiritalium interiora sermonum spiritu vivificante penetrari."
30. *De doctrina,* 3, 9(5).
31. *Ibid.,* 14-16(10).
32. *Ibid.,* 23(15).
33. Marrou, *op. cit.,* p. 490.
34. De Labriolle, *op. cit.,* p. 409. This passage is omitted in the English translation; see *Latin Christianity* (New York, 1924), p. 283. See Rand, *op. cit.,* pp. 85-90; F. Lot, *The End of the Ancient World,* trans. P. and M. Leon (New York, 1931), pp. 375-376.
35. *De doctrina,* 2, 9(7).

36. See Marrou, *op. cit.*, pp. 20-81; Rand, *op. cit.*, pp. 3-68; T. Haarhoff, *Schools of Gaul* (Oxford, 1920), pp. 151-197; P. Abelson, *The Seven Liberal Arts* (New York, 1906), pp. 1-71; G. Paré, A. Brunet, and P. Tremblay, *La renaissance du xiie siècle* (Paris and Ottawa, 1933), pp. 116-117.

37. *De doctrina*, 3, 34(24).

38. *Ibid.*, 36-37(25).

39. *Ibid.*, 40(29).

Chapter II

ILLUSTRATIONS OF THE
INFLUENCE OF AUGUSTINE'S
THEORY OF LITERATURE

AUGUSTINE'S axiom that the Christian will love "the truth in words, not words themselves" is repeated word for word in the ninth century by Rabanus Maurus: *in verbis verum amare, non verba,*[1] and Rabanus is only one of the many writers who repeated and developed what Augustine had set forth.[2] However, because the present chapter is illustrative, not systematic, in intention, it treats only a few representative writers.[3] Any systematic survey of the development of the Augustinian theory would have to include earlier figures like Eucherius of Lyons, Boethius, Cassiodorus, and a host of others who are considered perhaps to belong to the classical not to the medieval world of time. The *Formularum spiritalis intelligentiae* of Eucherius is a work of great importance because it sets forth in detail the exegetical principles of reading for underlying meaning and supplies for the student a dictionary of symbolic referents from the Bible. For just such a work Augustine asked in the *De doctrina*. The commentaries of Boethius on Aristotle and on Cicero have much that is valuable, and Cassiodorus in his *Institutiones* provides the practical monastic program for carrying out the schedule of Christian studies which Augustine had envisaged.[4]

The writers omitted here as well as and those to be considered repeat the refrain: since there can be no true pleasure apart from God, there can be no true beauty of the word, and no pleasure in the beautiful, apart from the truth. This truth to be loved and to be sought for behind the word is nothing vague; it is the simple and profound teaching of charity. In contrast to the clarity of dogmatic truth stand the frequent obscurities of the Bible, the word of God in human tongue. These obscurities hide the truth, but the allegorical method of interpretive reading supplies the means by which the obscure in Scripture may lead to the clear and evident. Furthermore, the discovery of hidden truth through the exertion of the mind is accompanied by true pleasure.

The Christian theory of interpretive reading made possible the preservation of pagan letters, for the Christian could see in Vergil's poetic mastery the sign, not of the Devil's charm, but of God's eloquence. In truth, the Christian felt that he alone could understand what Vergil was inspired to relate and prophesy; by interpreting it in the light of revelation, the Christian could restore

Vergil's poetry to its Master. The process was made easy because Vergil, like Homer, was understood by the grammarians to have had an allegorical purpose.[5] Servius Grammaticus says of the *Bucolics*, "The intention of the poet . . . in some places is that he give thanks to Augustus or other nobles by means of allegory."[6] The Christian commentator, revising the earlier commentary, had little more to do than transpose names: in the place of Vergil's allegorical referent, Caesar Augustus, the Christian had merely to substitute Christ, "for Vergil thought that the Sibyl prophesied Augustus, when actually all that she prophesied was concerning Christ."[7] In fact, as Fulgentius' *Mythology* shows, this method involved a systematic Christianizing of pagan myths and fables by interpreting them as allegories to be understood in the light of Christian revelation.[8] Many of the works of the great classical authors were saved to be employed for Christian use. Secular and sacred eloquence alike needed to be interpreted, so that the great models of classical literature as well as the Bible served to suggest to the medieval writer that the enigmatic, the difficult, the ambiguous, were part of the grand style of serious literature. The Christian understanding of the Bible and of pagan literature made almost inevitable the development of a theory that serious poetry should be allusive, enigmatic, periphrastic.

Isidore of Seville

Isidore states the principle clearly. For him the function of a poet is to create "fictions of speech." The Christian poet, having the Bible as his immediate or ultimate model, will be concerned with truth, and as a poet his office is to express the truth "obliquely, figuratively, with a certain beauty" (*obliquis figurationibus cum decore aliquo*).[9] In Isidore's phrase we have a clear reiteration of Augustine's principle that literary pleasure comes from the discovery of veiled truth; the combination of enigmatic fiction and clear underlying meaning may be taken as defining the beauty of poetry. The proper term for beauty thus defined appears to be *decor*. In the *Etymologiae* Isidore defines *decor* as the perfect, deriving from *decem*, ten. In the *Sententiae* he says that *decor* consists in the lovely (*pulchrum*) and the useful (*aptum*).[10] As De Bruyne points out, *decor* thus implies an intimate relationship between the good and the beautiful: "*Decor* considered for itself expresses the good, *decor* manifesting itself to the sight expresses the beautiful."[11] Isidore's use of the term, *decor*, is clearly Augustinian in inspiration, involving as it does the basic attitudes of enjoyment and utility. Only the truth is to be loved for itself; hence the enjoyment of loveliness is an aspect of the enjoyment of God, and in order to have such loveliness literature must be useful in leading man to the enjoyment of God. In a poem, fiction must be enjoyed obliquely, figuratively, so as to lead the mind to perceive the truth; the reader will then enjoy the sense of the beautiful. A poem is useful because it is beautiful.

Doctrine and Poetry

Vergil of Toulouse

To turn now rather sharply from the highway of the traditional figures to the byway of the obscure: in Vergil Maro, self-styled the Third, grammarian of Toulouse and enigmatic professor of the enigmatic, is to be found a clear illustration from an unexpected source of the influence of Augustinian principles of literature. Vergil lived perhaps in the sixth century and probably in Gaul. His only extant writings are two grammatical works, which may be characterized as obscurely systematic books of instruction in the enigmatic and difficult.[12] It is, of course, necessary to confess that not even the most basic things about Vergil can be determined. There is no telling when he is being humorous or whether he is ever humorous in intention, whether he was actually a learned man or merely a charlatan who took advantage of obscurity to hide his ignorance.[13]

Fortunately, the purpose of this chapter does not require that these doubts be resolved. It is necessary here only to show that Vergil reflects in his writing the Augustinian principles of literary theory. His very remoteness, his difference, the puzzle of his intent, will then serve to strengthen the postulate of Augustinian influence. To follow the main line of patristic succession from Augustine to Bede's successors of the Carolingian renaissance seems to circumscribe the evidence too narrowly. But to find an identity of theory between the sweet clarity of a Bede and the wild luxuriance of a Vergil Maro is to show that the theory had widespread influence. In Vergil, moreover, we consider a non-monastic, perhaps even a non-ecclesiastical figure, albeit one with a thoroughly Christian attitude.[14] He shared Augustine's view of pagan letters: they are to be used, but only for Christian purposes. Like Augustine, he subordinated his study to the understanding of Scripture.[15]

In the Preface to his *Epistolae,* Vergil, recounting the prophecy of a certain Tarquin who dwelled among the Persians, imitates the manner and the matter of the prophets. Vergil explains that his fable teaches allegorically that Scripture is the source of all man's spiritual knowledge and the model of his literary activity.[16] In his first *Epitome* he states the Augustinian principle that the end of literary effort is truth, the discovery of which through such effort being accompanied by pleasure.[17] He derives the principle from the etymology of the word *sapientia,* wisdom:

> Everywhere the accounting of our literature shows a profit because we [Christians] consider not the profit motive, but the search for wisdom. Moreover, *sapience* is derived from *savor* (*sapientia ex sapore*), because just as there is a certain savor in bodily taste, so also is there savor in the motion of the soul which may taste the sweetness of the liberal arts, which may discern the power of words and meanings, driving back the sour and truly following after the sweet. The sour we call whatever doctrines deny truth, the sweet whatever art and discipline promotes reason.[18]

Vergil's very method of establishing the principle is revealing. He seems almost to look inside the word to derive his meaning; its etymology has symbolic value. The end

33

of proper literary effort is sapience, and the attainment of sapience through such effort yields savor, the word from which sapience is derived. This etymological reasoning, itself in the Augustinian manner, in turn is followed by a development of the idea that all human learning and eloquence should serve the ends of Scripture.

But along with this clear presentation of the basic Augustinian doctrines of Christian poetics, Vergil of Toulouse develops the method of allegorical interpretation to the point where it becomes, as De Bruyne remarks, "an intellectual, aesthetic and mystic principle." [19] Vergil's system of forced interpretation through obscurity is not itself strange or remote, however; for even though Vergil carries the process to the dizzying point, the theory which he enunciates is, in all its parts, Augustinian in derivation. Thus Vergil justifies his practice of deliberately disarranging the normal succession of words, syllables, and letters on three counts: (1) it forces the mind to search for and discover an underlying meaning that is in accord with truth; (2) it gives the aesthetic pleasure that is derived from the strenuous discovery of the truth, and (3) it prevents the foolish from ignoring the profundity of divine truth because it is simply stated. [20]

Vergil of Toulouse gives in his grammatical writings the firmest evidence of the prevalence and development of the Augustinian theory. The practice he recommends is extreme, even wild. But Vergil reveals that Augustine's theoretical principles were taken with the greatest seriousness and were extended to apply to the practice of secular letters. The guide to such practice is to be found in Scripture: writer and reader are to search for the underlying meaning that is in accord with truth; they are to welcome the obscurity which, though it veils, yet leads to the pleasurable discovery of hidden truth.

Bede

Nothing could be further from the wildness of Vergil's grammatical work than the sweet reasonableness of Bede's little treatise, *De schematibus et tropis*.[21] Yet both derive from Augustine, the latter in direct fulfillment of Augustine's desire that learned men supply the Christian with needed instructional texts. In the *De schematibus et tropis* Bede classifies and analyzes what might be called devices of sentence structure (schemata) and figures of speech (tropes). Bede, possibly following the lead of Isidore of Seville, uses Donatus' selection of schemes and tropes and his arrangement, but the inspiration for his work is clearly Augustine.[22] Thus he begins with a statement of the difference as he understood it between Christian and pagan rhetoric:

Frequently for the sake of elegance in writing, words are ordered otherwise than in the manner of vulgar speech. This literary word-ordering, which the Greek grammarians call *schema*, we truly call *dress, form,* or *figure* because, through the means of the *schemes*, discourse, in a manner of speaking, is dressed and adorned. Moreover, tropes are found in such writing; that is, figures of speech, wherein, out of necessity or for ornament, the meaning of a word is transposed from its own meaning to one similar to, but not identical with, its usual or proper meaning. The Greeks, indeed, took pride in themselves for having discovered such figures or tropes. But, dearly beloved son, you and all who have desired to read this treatise, know that Holy Scripture is pre-eminent above other writings, not only in authority because it is divine, and in utility because it leads to eternal life, but also, finally, in antiquity and in its own original manner of discourse. Therefore, it has seemed good to me in a collection of examples to illustrate the fact that the masters of secular eloquence cannot lay claim to any form of the rhetorical usage, whether of *scheme* or *trope*, the use of which has not been anticipated in the Bible.[23]

Bede here demonstrates Augustine's point, fundamental to Christian rhetoric, that the Bible, because it is the word of God, is "in its authority, in its utility, in its antiquity," the model not only of the true, but of the beautiful in written speech as well. Such beauty as exists in the form of pagan eloquence derives its ultimate being from God, but the Bible is God's very word and, in whatever language it is properly translated, is the human image of divine eloquence. The Bible is therefore pre-eminent over all because it has the "authority" of divine inspiration, the power or "utility" to lead man to salvation, and the merit, in terms of human "antiquity," of being, as Bede thought, the first literature written by men.[24]

Bede's remark on the appropriateness of the word "dress" suggests that he subscribes to Augustine's theory that literature is eloquent, not in relation to its formal beauty, but in direct relation to its utility, its power to arouse the mind to an awareness of revealed truth. Because the pagan lacked faith he was limited to "verbal" eloquence; the Christian could penetrate to the truth which is not only the end, but the very cause of eloquence.

The basic Christian principle Bede has elsewhere derived from Christ's own teaching to His disciples when they asked Him why He spoke in parables (Matt. 13: 10-13): "He answered and said to them: because it is given you to know the mysteries of the kingdom of heaven, but to them it is not given. Who has, to him will be given, and he will abound; but who has not, from him will be taken away even that which he has." In his commentary on Matthew, Bede explains Christ's answer in detail. Those who "hear in parable" are those who consider only the "literal meaning." This they do "because their hearts are closed and they do not wish to know the truth." One who has only the love of the literal, the dress, really *has not* "because he has no love of hearing, nor seems he to possess anything either in natural ability or through literary exercise." He has nothing because he "rejoices not in the sweetness of true wisdom." Christ's words, for Bede, serve to establish the distinction between letter and spirit, the outward form and the inward meaning. Only the inner meaning has importance. Continuing with his explanation of Christ's teaching, Bede deduces from Christ's words the Augustinian theory of reading for underlying meaning. Reading should be slow and attentive, laborious, intent on the reward contained in the underlying meaning, "for often the simple man of studious inclinations enjoys what the careless man of talent misses." [25]

Doctrine and Poetry

Biblical exegesis supplies the tool to discover this inner meaning, and a treatise like Bede's *De schematibus* was designed, in part, as a technical aid for the student of the Bible. Moreover, the Bible is intended, as Bede believed, to serve as the model for all serious-minded discourse; therefore it was of primary importance that the rules of eloquence discovered, not invented, by the classical rhetoricians be established by illustrations from biblical practice. Bede is clearly guided by the *De doctrina;* Bede's treatise also reveals that he follows the lead of St. Augustine in accepting as his natural inheritance the forms of classical rhetoric.[26] Rhetorical theory, with important influences on literary theory and on habits of reading, is continuous from the rhetoricians of the Empire to those of the nineteenth century. Only in our century has the continuity been broken, so that now only the specially trained can follow without difficulty the subtleties of Bede's rhetorical refinements. Yet Bede's treatise is not intended for the expert or even for the advanced student of rhetoric; it is a list of basic devices that any proficient student should know.

The habits exercised in the old rhetorical discipline have lost all immediacy for us. How completely we have lost old rhetorical habits is suggested by the fact that for St. Augustine it was second nature to employ figures of rhetoric the very names of which have now been forgotten by all except the specialist. Augustine may even have felt that to write rhetorically, with full consciousness of the artificial ordering of his sentences, was more "natural" than to write without attention to such subtleties.

Even in his sermons and in works specially addressed to
the uneducated he cannot avoid contrivance.[27] Take al-
most at random a passage from the *De doctrina Chris-
tiana*, a reasonably straightforward expository work in
which Augustine is far from any purpose of elegant writ-
ing: "Prorsus haec est in docendo eloquentia, qua fit
dicendo, non ut libeat quod horrebat, aut quod fiat quod
pigebat, sed ut appareat quod latebat. . . . Bonorumque
ingeniorum insignis est indoles, in verbis verum amare,
non verba." [28]

Even to the rapid glance of the modern reader, the
conscious, artificial contrivance of the passage is obvious.
But unless he has studied, as a specialist, the schemata
of Donatus or Bede, he will tend to relate such style to
the esoteric. He will think of Joyce's *Ulysses*, not of
Lincoln's Gettysburg Address. In fact, Augustine is doing
no more than writing correctly, employing standard
schemata: *paranomasia, homeoteleuton, homeoptoton,
parhomeon, polyptoton*, all of which are considered by
Bede in the section of his treatise on the schemata. The
passage is not intended as a flight of rhetorical fancy
but as a piece of effective, sober exposition. Augustine,
like Lincoln, wished to convince, and he is very far from
wishing to impress. Unlike Joyce, Augustine is not ex-
ploring the unexplored possibilities of his language; on
the contrary, he is writing according to sharply defined
rules. His play with words is intended to make the reader
think not of the words, but of the truth within the words;
as he says in the passage itself, *in verbis verum amare,
non verba.*

39

Turning to Bede's illustrations of one of the more in-
teresting of the schemata, *paranomasia,* or wordplay in-
volving similarity of sound and difference of meaning,
we are at once impressed by the fact of how likely our
modern ear is to miss what must have seemed to Bede
a most obvious rhetorical pattern. In the then current
Vulgate reading of the sixth verse of Psalm 21, even the
attentive reader would now tend to ignore the wordplay,
which Bede gives as an obvious example of *paranomasia:*
"In te confisi sint, et non sunt confusi." Although the pair-
ing of *confisi-confusi* is striking, it remains true that we
would be as apt to overlook as we would be to notice
such wordplay. It is highly doubtful, indeed, that even
the very attentive reader could now be expected in the
course of ordinary reading to notice the figure in Philip-
pians 3:3, "Videte malos operarios, videte concisionem;
non autem sumus circumcisionem, qui spiritu Deo servi-
mus." For Bede the pairing *concisionem-circumcisionem*
is sufficiently obvious to be used as his second illustration
of *paranomasia.* To see the wordplay requires of us, at
the very least, an unusual kind of concentration. Our
habits of silent reading often place such stylistic details
beyond the threshold of conscious attention; but the
rhetorical training of our ancestors and their habit of
auditory reading tended to make them conscious of ver-
bal patterns. For, in fact, as any study of Bede on the
schemata will show, *paranomasia* is not by any means the
most subtle of the figures; it remains for us a figure which,
when noticed, appears deliberate. The habits of reading
encouraged by the study of the refinements of rhetoric

are an essential part of the literary judgment exercised by the pagan Roman and by his Christian successor as well.

But in Augustinian theory wordplay must serve a Christian purpose. Thus in the biblical examples of *paranomasia* which Bede gives, the Christian student, knowing the principles of the *De doctrina,* was expected to perceive that the wordplay helped to suggest an underlying meaning; for example, the wordplay balance, *confisi-confusi,* suggests the basic Christian antithesis between those who, confirmed (*confisi*) in God, possess Jerusalem and the *confusi,* who, not confirmed, possess Babylon, translated as *confusio* (confusion).

Bede's treatment of the schemes reveals the continuity of tradition in Augustinian rhetoric. His treatment of the tropes reveals the novel Christian element, probably because the tropes—metaphor, simile, allusion, allegory, parable—are more directly pertinent to the purpose of suggesting an underlying meaning than are the schemes. Therefore Bede differs from Donatus most sharply in his treatment of the tropes that are most directly concerned with the symbolic interpretation of the Bible. For example, the trope *synthesis,* although it is passed over briefly by Donatus, is most elaborately illustrated and discussed by Bede. Synthesis is the term applied to deliberate obscurity achieved by the transposition of words throughout a sentence or other period. Bede gives the example of a very obscure verse in Psalm 67, "Si dormiatis inter medios cleros pennae columbae deargentae *et cetera usque* nive dealbantur in Selmon." [29] To this

illustration he appends Augustine's detailed explanation
of the verse. This explanation occupies a full seventh of
the total number of pages Bede devotes to the entire sub-
ject of tropes, although synthesis is but one of the five
figures of hyperbaton, itself one of the thirteen tropes
considered by Donatus, Isidore, and Bede. This inordi-
nate attention given to one figure is to be explained simply
by the fact that to understand the verse at all, one must
actually interpret it. The verse defies literal translation;
it simply does not "make sense" on the literal level. To
elucidate its obscurity, as Augustine shows, one must re-
sort to figurative interpretation. But the figurative inter-
pretation in Augustine's hands does more than make
sense of the verse; it reveals as one underlying meaning
of the verse the divine promise that sins may be remitted
and that the blessed in Holy Church will triumph. Augus-
tine's extraordinary analysis of the verse emerges as a
notable model for Christian reading. The verse, with
Augustine's explanation of it, apparently stands for Bede
as a classical example of the dynamism of biblical ob-
scurity. The deliberate obscurity of the passage forces
the mind of the zealous reader in the very attempt at
understanding to rise to a perception of divine truth. As
Bede saw it, the figure in biblical usage served to connect,
by an inseparable union, outer form and inner meaning.
Its importance, then, lies in its illustration of the basic
principle of the Christian theory of literature, *in verbis
verum amare, non verba,* the perfect adaptation of outer
form to inner meaning.

The other trope to which Bede gives equal attention

is allegory. There is, needless to say, no counterpart to Bede's discussion in Donatus, since the development of allegorical interpretation, in its systematic form and with its widespread consequences, is essentially Christian. Under the impress of such men as Ambrose, Augustine, and Gregory, allegory became an indigenous part of the world view of Western Christendom, and men came to think not only of the Bible but also of the physical world and man's history in the world as a symbolic book written by the hand of God. The key to the interpretation of this book was the Christian Faith working on the revelation contained in the Bible—in short, in the commentary on Scripture. For this reason the biblical exegete had a sense of urgency like that felt, *mutatis mutandis,* by today's atomic scientist.

Since in biblical commentary the allegorical method was naturally of first importance, Bede gives not only examples of the five types of allegory, but also a long and detailed explanation of the allegorical method in general. He remarks first on the "substance" of allegory: "allegory is sometimes concerned with deeds, sometimes with words." By deeds (*facta*), Bede means historical events that are to be interpreted symbolically; by words (*verba*), he means expressions that are themselves metaphorical in Scripture. Of the first type he gives as an example Galatians 4:22, " 'For Abraham had two sons, one of a bondswoman, the other of a freewoman,' that is, the two testaments, as the Apostle explains." [30] The words themselves are not metaphorical, but the event has allegorical meaning. The second type he exemplifies in

Doctrine and Poetry

Isaiah 11:1, " 'The twig springs from the root of Jesse, and the flower from his root ascends'; in which is signified that the Lord Saviour was born of the tree of David through the Virgin Mary." As with the verse exemplifying synthesis, this verse, to be understood, must be interpreted. The meaning arises from the allegorical implication that Bede gives. Flower (*flos*) is a standard symbol for Christ. The root of Jesse symbolizes David and his descendants, among whom Mary is numbered. With the wordplay in the Latin words *virga* (twig) and *virgo* (virgin) the allegorical meaning may be completed: the twig (*virga*) of Jesse's root is the Virgin (*virgo*). It is thus we arrive at the underlying meaning indispensable to any understanding of what Ambrose calls prophetic enigma. "The Lord Saviour," Bede explains, "was born of the tree of David through the Virgin Mary." [31] Bede gives some further examples and then passes to a discussion of the levels of allegorical interpretation.

Delimitation of the possible levels of allegory serves not only to clarify the method, but also to limit the dangerous possibilities of individual interpretation by supplying a norm against which each interpretation may be checked. For example, if an interpreter sees in the verse from Isaiah just quoted the symbolic meaning that the Church could not live except on the branch of Jesse, that is, let us say, as an adjunct of the Synagogue, his obviously heretical interpretation is, as we shall see, on the allegorical level and can be refuted by reference to the established allegorical meaning of other passages. The levels, as Bede gives them, are the "historical, allegorical

or typical, tropological or moral, and the anagogical."
He cites Psalm 147:1, "Praise the Lord, Jerusalem,
praise your God, Sion." Jerusalem may be interpreted
on any of the four levels: "*Jerusalem* may rightly be
understood to concern on the historical level, the cities of
the earth; on the allegorical level, the Church of Christ;
on the tropological level, the blessed soul wheresoever it
is; on the anagogical level, the native land of heaven." [32]
Allegorically interpreted, the Bible serves the Christian
as an encyclopedic summary not only of the highest wis-
dom, but, quite literally, of all wisdom, since not only
the events and words of the Bible could be allegorically
interpreted, but all creation and all history as well.

Bede's treatise, which provided for the Christian poet
the specific suggestions lacking in the *De doctrina,* en-
ables us to perceive how allegory served as more than a
mere ornament and why the influence of the allegorical
method was everywhere felt in medieval literature. As
de Labriolle observes:

It was the allegorical interpretation of the Bible which ac-
customed Christian thinking to discover symbols everywhere,
to follow the pure spirit behind appearances, to see in each
form the evidence or clothing of a meaning. This mystic con-
viction, so different from the customary question of the sci-
ences, was to impose on generations of writers, of liturgists,
of artists, the task of deciphering the divine masterpiece in
which everything is a symbol, a teaching, a mystic fitness
which pious faith understands. [33]

Thus Bede's elaborate explanation of the allegorical
method most clearly reveals the specifically Christian
aspect of his rhetorical ideas. [34] Bede's *De schematibus et*

tropis, in purpose and in what it adds to the basic work of Donatus, is based on the theory expounded in the *De doctrina.*

Alcuin

The writers of the Carolingian period (except for Erigena), although they are later than Bede, are so directly of his school as to throw considerable light in retrospect on the Augustinian theory as it was developed in England and brought to the continent by Alcuin, the master of Charlemagne's court school. An Englishman in the direct tradition of Bede, he gives further evidence of the continuing influence of Augustine's theory of literature. Charlemagne himself seems deeply imbued with the Augustinian ideal, for in one of his letters he clearly expresses the principles of biblical pre-eminence and of the utility of literary study. The latter is to be encouraged, he says, "so that those who desire to please God by living rightly may also not neglect to please Him by rightly speaking; for it is written: *'by your words you will be saved and by your words you will be condemned'* (Matt. 12:37)." The study of letters has as its purpose increase in ability to understand the underlying meaning of Scripture. Charlemagne speaks in echo of his spiritual master:

> And well do we all know that however dangerous are the errors of the letter the errors of meaning are much more dangerous. Wherefore we urge you not only not to neglect the study of the letter, but also in the most humble intention of pleasing God hastily to learn this, so that the more easily and directly you may be able to penetrate to the mystery of divine

46

Scriptures. Moreover, since in the sacred pages are found *schemes, figures, tropes,* and the rest like to these, there can be no doubt that anyone reading will understand the underlying meaning (*spiritualiter*) the more readily the more fully he has first been instructed in the mastery of the letter.[35]

The man directly responsible for these educational directives to which Charlemagne gave the weight of his authority was probably Alcuin, who sets forth the traditional doctrine at the beginning of his *Grammatica.* To find wisdom one must desire it "because of God . . . not for the sake of man's praise." The way to wisdom, he says, begins formally with the study of the liberal arts. He cites in support of this Proverbs 9:1, "Wisdom built a house for himself; hewed out seven columns." The underlying meaning (*sententia*) of the verse pertains to the Incarnation of Christ or to the Church, and finally to the part that the seven liberal arts play in wisdom: "The wisdom of the liberal disciplines of the letter is established in the seven columns." Perfect knowledge (*scientia*) is impossible "except as one is raised up through these seven columns or grades." Through the seven "grades" of the liberal arts one approaches the heights of biblical wisdom. Alcuin establishes the traditional relationship in Christian culture between a sense of the continuity of literary tradition and the new orientation of all learning toward Scripture. What has given light to pagan darkness the Augustinian Christian will not reject.[36]

In his *Rhetoric,* an imaginary dialogue between himself and Charlemagne, Alcuin reaffirms the distinction between use and enjoyment, fundamental to Augustine's *De doctrina.* "Virtue, knowledge, truth, love of good," he says, "are so illustrious and noble that they should be loved and followed" because of their inherent excellence. But since the Christian and the pagan alike cherish these virtues, what, Charlemagne asks, "is the difference between these philosophers and the Christians?" Alcuin's simple reply, "Faith and Baptism," sums up the fundamental principle that Christian doctrine reveals the valid end of rhetoric, as of all literary endeavor, to be the enjoyment of God, the source of all virtue. Alcuin now proceeds to a survey of the cardinal virtues in the light of the Christian Faith. Charlemagne then asks what is the end aimed at in the practice of virtue. Alcuin replies, "The object is to love God and our neighbors," and he continues with an eloquent reaffirmation of the central Christian thesis that the good things of this world, among which eloquence is to be numbered, are not to be enjoyed for themselves but are to be used for the purpose of enjoying God:

> What is easier than to love forms beauteous to the sight, tastes . . . sounds . . . odors . . . objects, and all the honors and amenities of a lifetime? Wherefore is it easier for our soul to cherish these things, which disappear like unsubstantial shadows, and not love God, who is eternal beauty and enduring sweetness and unending pleasure . . . particularly since the Sacred Scriptures require only that we love God and our Lord with our whole heart and our whole soul and our whole mind, and that we love our neighbor as ourself? . . . To love the things of this world is more difficult than to love Christ; for what the soul longs for in this world is happiness and

permanence, and these it does not find, because every good thing here below recedes and disappears.[37]

De Bruyne says concerning the passage, "In this significant page, Alcuin admits . . . an aesthetic sensibility associated with the love of the Good, with the instinct of happiness, with the desire for eternity." [38] In short, Alcuin here reiterates the basic premise of Augustinian poetic theory.

Rabanus

Rabanus Maurus, disciple of Alcuin, shows even more clearly than his master the continuity of the Augustinian tradition. His great work, the *De universo,* an expansion and development of Isidore's *Etymologiae,* fulfills Augustine's wish that some man of learning might classify and explain "places, animals, plants, trees, stones, or unknown metals and other such species as are mentioned in Scripture." [39] Rabanus arranges his work "so that the prudent reader will find continuously ordered the historical and mystical, literal and figurative explanation of individual matters." [40] Thus the *De universo* provides a basic tool for interpretive reading.

Augustine's *De doctrina,* in fact, actually reappears in somewhat modified form in Book III of Rabanus' *De clericorum institutione,* where he discusses "how what is written in Scripture ought to be studied and taught and also what in the studies and arts of the pagans are useful for the ecclesiastic to examine." In particular Rabanus deals (Chs. 3-15) with the purposeful obscurity of the Bible and outlines the Augustinian method for dealing with this obscurity (Bks. II and III of the *De doctrina*).[41] He stresses Augustine's solution to the problem of biblical obscurity and restates the principle that the discovery of truth in the obscure is accompanied by pleasure. He observes that no one would readily follow the indirect path to underlying meaning unless there was pleasure in the difficult unraveling of meaning. He quotes Augustine: "No one wanders through similes in order to understand more readily; rather those things sought with some difficulty are found the more pleasingly." [42]

The ultimate source of this literary pleasure is charity, the love of God, for to discover truth is to approach God, and to approach Him is to love Him; that is why "no one knows perfectly unless he loves rightly." [43] Rabanus concludes this portion of his treatise with a specific reference, in Chapter 15, to the *De doctrina:* "Let one who wishes to know more fully concerning these things seek and he will find them in St. Augustine's *De doctrina christiana* whence we have excerpted them." [44]

The final chapters of Rabanus' *De clericorum institutione* (18-39) correspond in function to Book IV of the *De doctrina,* which sets forth the techniques of expounding Scripture. Rabanus characteristically includes a discussion of the seven liberal arts, which Augustine left to others. His instructions in teaching, although they rest heavily on Augustine, are somewhat modified in being directed specifically to the needs of the preacher. Of some passing interest is Rabanus' definition of grammar as "the science of interpreting poets and writers of fact and the science of the order of writing and speaking truly." [45] In the first part of the definition Rabanus expresses the distinction, which we have previously met in Isidore, between writers of poetic fiction and writers of fact. The purpose of the former, as we recall, is to express the truth "obliquely, figuratively, with a certain beauty." One function of grammar is to teach the student how to interpret the figurative so that he may discover the underlying truth. In addition, grammar teaches both the poet and writer of fact to write "truly," that is, "for the truth in words, not for the words themselves." Grammar has a regular and honorable place in Christian schools as long as it teaches not words but the right use of words. [46] Indeed, grammar is essential because of its value in the study of the Bible. For example, the schemes and tropes studied in grammar are found illustrated in the Bible. "It is necessary to understand these," says Rabanus, recalling *De doctrina,* "in order that the difficulties in Scripture may be resolved when the meaning of the words is absurd if taken literally." [47] As Augustine had pointed out, knowledge of the schemes and tropes enables the reader to discover the underlying truth in the obscurity of the biblical letter.

The study of metrics Rabanus also defends on the grounds that many types of verse are found in Scripture and in Christian poetry. The study of the "poems and books of the pagans" may be undertaken "because of the flower of eloquence" in them, but such works must be purified by the light of revelation. The authority for and the method of such purification is to be found in St.

Jerome's allegorical interpretation of Deuteronomy 21: 10-14, verses which set forth the procedure for purifying captive women. The procedure, says Rabanus, interpreted not "according to the letter, which is ridiculous," but allegorically according to Jerome, is the guide to handling "the pagan poets and pagan books of earthly wisdom." We cut away what is "superfluous concerning idols, love, care for earthly things, and convert to our doctrine what we find useful in them." Apart from affording authority for the propriety of using pagan literature, the allegorical interpretation of the verses affords an illustration of the methods to be employed in "purifying" pagan letters to make them fit for use. Like the Bible itself, pagan letters are to be interpreted allegorically where they conflict with Christian doctrine.[48] Rabanus then makes clear the usefulness of eloquence based on a clear understanding of the pre-eminence of the Bible by repeating Augustine's dictum on the true basis of eloquence: "in words to love truth, not words." [49]

Scotus Erigena

The influence of Augustinian theory may finally be illustrated from John Scotus Erigena, who is often assumed to be a distinctly original theologian. He has been called an isolated figure not really to be measured in the terms of the "dominant Augustinianism of the early Middle Ages." [50] Yet nowhere is the Augustinian theory of aesthetic pleasure better illustrated than in his example (in *De divisione naturae*) of two men looking at the same beautiful object. One man is torn by temporal desires; the other is a wise man who is above such desires. Both look at the beautiful object, "receive the image in their bodily sense, imprint it on the memory, consider it in thought." Here all resemblance ceases. The worldling desires the object and is filled with cupidity. The wise man "connects the beauty of the object with the praise of the Creator" and thus uses the temporal object with a view toward the enjoyment of God. He experiences true pleasure. The worldling attempts to enjoy the object for itself, misuses it, and is discomfited.[51] The perception of beauty is at one with the perception of truth: aesthetic pleasure is an adjunct of charity.

In his *Expositiones super hierarchiae caelesten S. Dionysii*, Erigena also reveals fundamental agreement with the details of the Augustinian theory about the purposes of the obscure and the figurative in the Bible. They exist for the purpose of exercising the mind, of purifying it so that it may be prepared to share in the joy of revealed truth. He says that if one reads "the prophetic fictions" literally, without attempting the ascent to "the contemplation of intelligible things of which these are the images, not only will the soul not be purified and exercised but will even be most wickedly stained and most foolishly oppressed."[52] The figurative has as its purpose for Erigena, as for Augustine, the exercise and purification of the soul or mind so that it may attain the understanding of revealed truth with its accompanying pleasure. The beauty of the figurative lies not in the figure itself but in the discovery of what the figure repre-

53

sents, "for what is more lowly than the mustard seed and
what more precious than the power in it, since indeed
it is compared not only to the Catholic faith but even
to Christ Himself, as the evangelical parable teaches." [53]
Erigena derives the same idea from St. Paul's "the letter
kills"; this applies, he believes, "generally to all the spirit-
ual figures, whether in words, in deeds or in the images
of sensible things set forth in the whole course of divine
Scriptures, through which the truth of spiritual things
and the arcane mystery of the supermundane are signified
to the end of exercising the human soul and conducting
it from earthly things to heaven." [54] The obscurities of
Scripture have also the purpose of preventing "the pure,
light-filled, healthful beauty of the invisible pearls being
cast before swine." [55] Erigena's statement that the truth
of underlying meaning is, like the pearl, to be guarded
from the unillumined swine suggests very clearly the
influence of the *De doctrina.*

In the *Expositiones,* Erigena makes clear the connec-
tion of the "theological" with the "poetic" figures. They
have basically the same purpose, a principle obviously
deriving from the axiom that the Bible is the basic model
of all literary activity:

> The poetic art gives moral or natural teaching by means of
> imaginary fictions and allegorical analogies in order to exer-
> cise the human spirit: this is the proper function of heroic
> poets who praise figuratively the deeds and customs of heroes.
> Thus theology, like poetry, has Holy Scripture by means of
> fictional imaginings address our souls and lead them from the
> external, corporal senses, to the perfected understanding of

54

intelligible things, as if from an imperfect puerile understanding to a maturity of the inner man.[56]

Erigena here gives the theoretical basis for the adoption of enigmatic, obscure style in the writing of poetry and for the concomitant habit of interpretive reading. Except for the most practical matters, writing had, of necessity, to exercise the mind or it could not serve any but an improper purpose.

If we may judge from the evidence of the writers here considered, Augustine's concept of literature as consisting of a shell (the letter) and a core (the sentence) became a commonplace of medieval literary theory. Structural and figurative difficulties of the letter were felt to have direct relation to aesthetic pleasure, which derives from the discovery of truth in the underlying meaning. Enigmatic poetry can give to the reader a fresh and vigorous perception of the truth because his mind has been prepared by interpretive exercise. If the poet imparts such fresh and powerful insight, he, in theory, succeeds in giving aesthetic pleasure.

This theoretical view of the purpose of literature explains the serious and widespread interest of the early Middle Ages in riddles, by moderns reduced to a place in children's books or in adult games. Aldhelm, Tatwin, Eusebius, to mention only English names, were distinguished churchmen who wrote riddles in all seriousness.[57] Their activity seems to us childish or simply puzzling until we remember that for them all created things—even the lowly mustard seed—had symbolic significance. They

believed that to ponder words or facts in order to arrive at the reality behind the attribute was to exercise the noblest function of the mind. And their interest in riddles is to be explained by the importance they placed on the enigmatic. Not only riddles but also other literary phenomena of the early Middle Ages are thus to be explained; for example, in the eyes of the writer of the esoteric and obscure kind of composition called Hesperic Latin, "every poem to be beautiful seems to have to be a problem to solve." [58] This Latin represents not wild Irish madness but, like the writing of Vergil of Toulouse, simply an extreme development of the basic theory which saw in obscurity a means to exercise the mind so that it might be prepared for the aesthetic perception of the truth. The serious composition of riddles and the composition of Hesperic Latin are symptoms of the operative prevalence of the Augustinian theory of literature.

NOTES TO CHAPTER II

1. See below, nn. 28 and 49.
2. Rand, *op. cit.*, p. 251.
3. See Vol. I of E. de Bruyne's *Etudes d'esthétique médiévale* (Brussels, 1946); for special studies of Augustine's aesthetic see K. Svoboda, *L'Esthétique de Saint Augustin et ses sources* (Brno, 1933), and E. Chapman, *Saint Augustine's Philosophy of Beauty* (New York, 1939); neither work is entirely satisfactory.
4. Eucherius has been cited above (Ch. I, n. 22). See Rand, *op. cit.*, pp. 135-180, for Boethius; and for Cassiodorus see C. W. Jones, *An Introduction to Divine and Human Readings* (New York, 1946). Gregory the Great is omitted because of his disposition to look with a jaundiced eye at the practice of letters. His contribution to biblical exegesis is as fundamental as that of Augustine. Reference is made to his great work, the *Moralia,* in Ch. III; see nn. 44-46.
5. See Marrou, *op. cit.*, pp. 495 ff.
6. *In Virgilii bucolicon librum commentarius,* ed. G. Thilo and H. Hagen (Leipzig, 1902), Vol. 3, Pt. I, p. 2.
7. Iunii Philargyrii Grammatici, *Explanatio in bucolica Vergilii,* in Thilo and Hagen, *op. cit.*, Pt. II, p. 78; "Virgo id est Iustitia vel Maria. Redit id est post Evam. . . . *Nova Progenies* id est Augustum dicit. Aestimavit enim Virgilius, quod de Augusto praedixit Sibylla, cum de Christo omnia prophetavit." The commentary is sometimes attributed to the Irish monk, Adamnus. See M. Roger, *L'enseignement des lettres classiques d'Ausone à Alcuin* (Paris, 1905), pp. 262 and 266.
8. In *Opera,* ed., R. Helm (Leipzig, 1898), pp. 3-80.
9. *Etymologiae,* ed., W. Lindsay (Oxford, 1911), VIII, vii.
10. *Ibid.,* X, xviii; *Sententiae,* 8.18, *PL,* 83, 551: "Decor elementorum omnium in pulchro et apto consistit; sed pulchrum ei quod se ipsum est pulchrum, ut homo ex anima et membris omnibus constans. Aptum vero est, ut vestimentum et victus. Ideoque hominem dici pulchrum ad se, quia non vestimento et victui est homo necessarius, sed ista homini; ideo autem illa apta, quia non sibi, sicut homo, pulchra, aut ad se, sed ad aliud, id est,

ad hominem accomodata, non sibimet necessaria." See De Bruyne, *op. cit.,* pp. 95-97.

11. De Bruyne, *op. cit.,* p. 81.
12. Virgilii Maronis, *Opera,* ed. J. Huemer (Leipzig, 1890). D. Tardi, *Les Epitomae de Virgile de Toulouse* (Paris, 1928), contains an edition of the *Epitomae,* with a valuable French translation.
13. See Roger, *op. cit.,* pp. 110-126; F. Raby, *A History of Secular Latin Poetry in the Middle Ages* (Oxford, 1934), I, 153 ff. De Bruyne, *op. cit.,* pp. 115-120, reports Tarde (*sic*) as characterizing Vergil, "Provincial vaniteux, ébloui, fanatisé par les maîtres de sa petite ville." Tardi actually offers this as one of several possible readings of Vergil's character and position. The quotation is followed in Tardi by a question mark. His own opinion is very different: "Puisse-t-on y trouver la preuve que l'enseignement de Virgile, trop bafoué ou trop exalté par les critiques, remplit un rôle d'intermédiare entre le passé et l'avenir, et qu'il constitue un des chaînons du lien qui rattache la littérature latine expirante à la renaissance carolingienne."
14. Tardi, *op. cit.,* p. 24.
15. In *Opera,* Huemer, *op. cit.,* pp. 135-136.
16. *Ibid.,* pp. 105-106.
17. *Ibid.,* p. 3.
18. *Ibid.,* p. 4.
19. De Bruyne, *op. cit.,* p. 119. In this "wildness" De Bruyne seeks to establish an "asiatic" or "baroque" medieval tradition, distinct from true classical practice. The difference is largely a matter of extremes, not of fundamental disagreement.
20. *Ibid.,* p. 76. Vergil places the argument in the mouth of a certain Aeneas, "who first among us was wont to divide locutions." Whoever Aeneas was, and whatever the strangeness of practice that follows from his rhetorical principles, he appears to speak from the *De doctrina,* 4, 22(9), where Augustine gives the reasons impelling the sacred writers to an obscurity which is "useful and healthy." Aeneas, or his follower, Vergil, at any rate, apparently interpreted good literary health in a Joycean or even Pickwickian sense, but Aeneas' reasons for obscurity are identical with those of Augustine, who says: "ad exercendas et eliminandas quodammodo mentes legentium, et ad rupenda fastidia atque acuenda studia discere uolentium, celandos quoque, sive ut ad

pietatem convertantur, sive ut a mysteriis secludantur, animos impiorum."

21. In *Rhetores Latini minores,* ed. C. Halm (Leipzig, 1863), pp. 607-618.

22. Donatus, *Ars majora,* ed. H. Keil, *Grammatii Latini,* IV (Leipzig, 1819), 397-402; Isidore of Seville, *Etymologiae,* Lindsay, *op. cit.,* I, xxxvi-xxxvii. Isidore follows Donatus quite closely, sometimes explaining more fully than Donatus, sometimes supplying his own examples.

23. Halm, *op. cit.,* p. 607.

24. The importance of this principle and its significance for a proper understanding of Bede's treatise may be overlooked. See E. Curtius, *Europäische Literatur und lateinisches Mittelalter* (Bern, 1948), pp. 54-55.

25. In *Matthaei evangelium expositio, PL,* 92, 66.

26. For a brilliant discussion of the relation between Christian and classical culture see Marrou, *op. cit.,* pp. 342-404 and *passim.* See M. Helin, *Medieval Latin Literature,* trans. T. Snow (New York, 1949), p. 5; De Labriolle, *op. cit.,* pp. 11-13.

27. Augustine was fully aware of the impress of his rhetorical training on his habits of writing. See Rand, *op. cit.,* p. 275. See Marrou, *op. cit.,* pp. 76-83; C.-I. Balmus, *Etude sur le style de Saint Augustine* (Paris, 1930), pp. 187-305; M. Comeau, *La Rhétorique de Saint Augustine d'aprés les Tractatus in Ioannem* (Paris, 1930), pp. 46-70; A. Régnier, *De la latinité des sermons de Saint Augustin* (Paris, 1886), pp. 115-156. There is a special study of Augustine's use of wordplay in his sermons: C. Mohrmann, "Das Wortspiel in der Augustinischen Sermones," *Mnemosyne,* 3d ser., III (1935-1936), 33-61.

28. *De doctrina,* 4, 11(36). For the style of the *De doctrina,* see M. Sullivan, *De doctrina Christiana Liber Quartus* (Washington, 1930), pp. 31-41.

29. Halm, *op. cit.,* pp. 614-615. "*Si dormiatis inter medios cleros pennae columbae deargentatae* et cetera usque *nive dealbabuntur in Selmon.* Prius enim hic, ut Augustinus ait, quaerendus est ordo verborum, quo modo finiatur sententia, quae utique pendet, cum dicitur 'si dormiatis.' . . . Potest et sic intelligi, ut in eo quod dictum est 'pennae columbae deargentatae' subaudiatur 'eritis,' ut iste sit sensus: 'Vos qui tamquam spolia speciei domus dividimini, si dormiatis inter medios cleros, pennae columbae

deargentatae eritis, id est, in altiora elevabimini, conpagini tamen ecclesiae cohaerentes.' . . . Magnum itaque aliquod bonum est dormire inter medios cleros, quae nonnulli duo testamenta esse voluerunt, ut dormire sit inter medios cleros in eorum testamentorum auctoritate requiescere, id est, utriusque testamenti testimoniis adquiescere, ut quando aliquid ex his profertur et probatur, omnis intentio pacifica quiete finiatur."

30. *Ibid.*, p. 616.
31. *Ibid.* A combination of word and fact is possible: "Aliquando factis simul et verbis una eademque res allegorice significatur." For the interpretation of Isaiah, see Jerome, *PL*, 24, 147-148.
32. Halm, *op. cit.*, p. 617: "Allegory," indicating both the general and the specific, leads to confusion; however, Bede's term, *typicum*, was not generally used. I have translated it "allegorical," a term already in use as early as Eucherius of Lyons. (See his *Formularum spiritalis intelligentiae, PL*, 50, 728.)
33. De Labriolle, *op. cit.*, pp. 408-409. See also pp. 351 and 406.
34. The final trope which Bede considers is homeosis; that is, comparison. The trope has three subdivisions: image, parable and example. Obviously, the trope is concerned directly with the revelation of meaning but actually needs little explanation. The three tropes—comparison, transposition, allegory—serve as models for serious writing that is based on the Bible. They are means for leading the reader to a deeper understanding of the truth through the need to interpret what is said on the surface.
35. *De litteris colendis*, ed. P. Lehmann, *Fuldaer Studien* (Sitzungsber.-Bayer., Akad., philos.-philol. u. hist. Kl., 1927), pp. 8-9. The text in *PL*, 98, 895-897, is poor; that in the *MGH* is based on a later MS.
36. *Grammatica, PL*, 101, 850-854.
37. S. Howell, *The Rhetoric of Alcuin* (Princeton, 1941), pp. 145-153; see also p. 63. Professor Howell's translation is used.
38. De Bruyne, *op. cit.*, p. 195. See also pp. 226-229 for his account of the interesting Carolingian commentary on Horace: "Il est, en effet, impossible de bien écrire si on ne pense pas juste: comme dit Horace (et nôtre auteur y insiste longuement): 'recte scribere procedit ex sapere.'"
39. *De doctrina*, 3, 59(39).
40. "Praefatio," *PL*, 111, 9-13.
41. *PL*, 107, 296-379.

42. *Ibid.*, 380, *De doctrina*, 2, 7-8(6). De Bruyne, *op. cit.*, p. 339, apparently agrees with H. Glunz, *Die Literarästhetic des europäischen Mittelalters* (Bochum, 1937), pp. 43 ff., that Rabanus shows "a genuine originality" in setting forth his solution to the problem of biblical obscurity. The passage cited by De Bruyne in evidence of this "originality" consists simply in a transcription by Rabanus of the *De doctrina!* Rabanus himself specifically disclaims originality in the "Praefatio": "Nec per me quasi ex me ea protuli, sed auctoritati innitens majorum, per omnia illorum vestigia sum secutus." (See also his statement of indebtedness to the *De doctrina*, below, n. 44.) The failure to keep in mind the centrality of Augustine in the patristic tradition has led Glunz and De Bruyne into unnecessary complications. The basic literary theory is permanent but is modified to include new situations or particular problems. Santayana's Spanish proverb, quoted by Rand, *op. cit.*, p. 251, should be kept in mind.

43. *PL,* 107, 382: "Quia nemo perfecte sapit, nisi is qui recte diligit . . . quantum perficit in sapientia, tantum in charitate."

44. *Ibid.*, 392.

45. *Ibid.*, 395.

46. *Ibid.* "Inculpabiliter enim, imo laudabiliter hanc artem discit, quisquis in ea non inanem pugnam verborum diligit facere, sed rectae locutionis scientiam et scribendi peritiam habere appetit."

47. *Ibid.*

48. *Ibid.*, 396: "Poemata autem et libros gentilium si velimus propter florem eloquentiae legere, typus mulieris captivae tenendus, quam Deuteronomium describit; et Dominum ita praecepisse commemorat, ut si Israelites eam habere vellet uxorem, calvitium ei faciat, ungues praesecet, polos auferat, et cum munda fuerit effecta, tunc transeat in uxoris amplexu. Haec si secundum litteram intelligimus, nonne ridicula sunt? Itaque et nos hoc facere solemus, hoc que facere debemus, quando poetas gentiles legimus, quando in manus nostras libri veniunt sapientiae saecularis, si quid in eis utile reperimus, ad nostrum dogma convertimus; si quid vero superfluum de idolis, de amore, de cura saecularium rerum, haec radamus, his calvitium inducamus, haec in unguium more ferro acutissimo desecemus. Hoc tamen prae omnibus cavere debemus, ne haec licentia nostra offendiculum fiat infirmis: ne pereat qui infirmus est in scientia nostra frater, propter quem Christus mortuus est, si viderit in idolio recumbentes." The interpretation

of the passage is that of St. Jerome, from the famous Epistle 70, ed. I. Hilberg, *CSEL*, LIV, p. 702. The obscurity of the Bible had as one of its purposes keeping the unlearned from truths the expression of which they could not understand. Rabanus' final warning to those competent to read the pagan writers has the same practical basis.

49. *PL*, 107, 406-408: "Est autem optimus modus dicendi, qui fit ut qui audit, verum audiat; et quae audi, intelligat; bonorumque ingeniorum insignis est indoles, in verbis verum amare, non verba."

50. M. Cappuyns, *Jean Scot Erigene* (Louvain, 1933), p. 384.

51. *PL*, 122, 827. De Bruyne, *op. cit.*, pp. 364-370, states excellently the basic tenor of Erigena's argument: "Seul l'art qui élève l'âme à l'activité raisonnable de la vertu et dont la jouissance est rapportée à l'amour de l'ineffable Beauté de Dieu peut se justifier aux yeux de la sagesse parfaîte." But, failing perhaps to heed the context of the illustration, which is concerned with the problem of the tree of the knowledge of good and evil, De Bruyne wishes to see, in Erigena's words, a description of "l'attitude esthétique opposée à l'attitude pratique." But Erigena's purpose is precisely to show that the one object produces both an evil and a good effect. The good effect is itself practical, useful, inasmuch as it leads to the thought of God. Augustine's doctrine of utility and enjoyment provides the clue to the understanding of the passage.

52. *PL*, 122, 145.

53. *Ibid.*, 150.

54. *Ibid.*, 171.

55. These are the words of "Dionysius." (See Erigena's translation, *PL*, 122, 1044.)

56. *Expositiones, PL*, 122, 146.

57. De Bruyne, *op. cit.*, p. 148, makes a misleading distinction—following modern aesthetic theory—between the love of the enigmatic and the search for truth. Speaking of Aldhelm he says, "Chez Aldhelm, comme chez les autres auteurs, l'amour profane de la devinette s'associe avec la passion religieuse du sens mystique: le poète s'amuse aux énigmes du savoir naturel, le moine conseille la recherche des quatre sens de l'Ecriture." It is not only more exact but more to the point to say that the Christian, because he believed in revealed truth, found oneness of pleasure and truth in discovering the underlying meaning of all he saw and read.

58. De Bruyne, *op. cit.*, p. 126. See E. K. Rand, "The Irish Flavor of Hesperica Famina" in *Ehrengabe K. Strecker* (Dresden, 1931), pp. 134-143. See the edition and translation of the *Hesperica* by F. Jenkinson (Cambridge, 1908). The *Hesperica* also appears in A. Mai, *Classicorum Auctorum*, V, 479-500, an old but valuable collection of early medieval Latin documents, including Vergil of Toulouse, Aldhelm, and many others. See M. Manitius, *Geschichte de lateinischen literature des Mittelalters*, I (Munich, 1911), 156-160; Roger, *op. cit.*, pp. 238-256.

Chapter III

THE PRACTICE OF
CHRISTIAN POETRY:
ALDHELM AND BEDE

IN the Christian culture formulated in the *De doctrina,*
a place is made for the practice of letters. The flourishing
of Latin poetry in the fourth and fifth centuries testifies
to a lively willingness to take advantage of the oppor-
tunity. The writing of Christian Latin poetry—allowing
for the upheavals of the period of Germanic settlement
—is continuous to the Carolingian renaissance and be-
yond. Even Gregory, with his violent distrust of literary
activity, wrote hymns. Latin poetry, by no means re-
stricted to practical use in the liturgy, was composed in
Gaul, in Ireland, in England. Of the ecclesiastical writers
of the Carolingian renaissance Cappuyns says that "each
gave himself with passion to poetry; one can say, not a
cultivated man was there who did not practice it." [1] Of

this poetry in general may be said what has already been said of the Augustinian theory of literature: it reconciled —or at least juxtaposed—two apparently divergent interests, one in preserving the traditions of classical poetry, the other in promoting the ideals and dogma of the Christian Faith. A central problem of the Christian Latin poet was the relation of his poetry to its pagan prototype; or, in Augustinian terms, his problem consisted in learning how to *use* the form and diction of traditional pagan verse for the Christian purpose of celebrating charity.

In the work of assimilation the Christian poet had a basic problem: how to adapt an originally pagan vocabulary to the needs of Christian connotation. Isidore of Seville indicates an awareness of the problem. His *Etymologiae* and his *De differentiis* are basically an attempt to form a rich and useful Christian vocabulary. As Roger points out, "His constant care is to fix exactly the meaning of certain Latin words, serving to designate the ideas essential to Christian belief. Such words as *animus* and *anima, fides, spes* and *charitas, amor* and *dilectio,* clearly do not have the same meaning which the pagans gave to them." [2] The Bible, as Isidore indicated, was the basic storehouse for new connotations. It was also the arbiter of meaning. Such epithets as *Judex, Dux, Rex, Princeps, Dominus,* applied to God from the beginning, were little else than Latin translations of Biblical epithets.

The formation of a symbolic vocabulary was not a mere matter of language; it was a means of extending the range of the most necessary knowledge a Christian could have, the knowledge of God's purpose as it was revealed in the

words of the Bible and the things of the Book of Crea-
tion. To understand the spiritual meaning behind words
and things was to live, not to understand was to die. The
task of the Christian writer was defined in Paul's prescrip-
tion: "The letter kills, but the spirit vivifies." As even
the most cursory reading of the Fathers will show, the
work of forming the necessary Christian vocabulary of
words rich in spiritual connotations was under way from
the beginning. By the time of Eucherius of Lyons' treatise
on the spiritual meaning of words, cited above, the work
of semantic adaptation had proceeded to the point that
it was possible for him to write a synoptic, but fairly
complete, dictionary of symbolic significations, not only
for key words from the Bible, but also for the objects
of the natural world, animate and inanimate. It was now
possible for the Christian, in speaking, for example, of
a lion or of a deer, to mean Christ.[3] This connotative pos-
sibility was of great significance to the poet, and we find
in the fifth century a poem attributed to Orientius, the
Explanatio nominum domini, which consists of a list of
almost fifty symbolic names for Christ, with explanations
of the import and connotation of each. The epithets them-
selves are most various, ranging from "Lion" to "Dove";
from "King," "Prince," or "Duke of the Celestial Host"
to "Bridegroom" or "Boy"; from "Sun," "Star," "Rock,"
"Pearl" to the abstract epithet "Wisdom." [4]

Moreover, as has already been noted, the very diction
of pagan poetry was being made useful for Christian
purposes in the allegorization of Vergil and in the
thoroughgoing adaptation of pagan myth to Christian

meaning by Fulgentius.[5] A very early example of a Latin poet's adaptation of the names of pagan deities to the purposes of Christian symbol may be found in the *Phoenix*, attributed to Lactantius, concerning a mythological bird that is renewed in its own ashes, an allegorical representation of the Resurrection of Christ and of the just.[6] In the *Phoenix*, the Lord is symbolized under the figure of Phoebus, the Sun, a common epithet for Christ. The Phoenix worships this "radiant Lord"; it is alone admitted "to the secrets of Phoebus." The bird is likewise above the desires of the flesh, which are represented as the "chains of Venus," and "Death is its Venus, for alone in death is its pleasure."[7] The same conscious effort at adaptation is illustrated in Proba, whose purpose in writing the *Cento* was to show how Vergil's verses could be "changed for the better through divine meaning."[8] Whatever else the poem served to accomplish, it did make clear that Aurora, Olympus, Tartarus, and the rest of the pagan, Vergilian vocabulary could be used by Christian writers. Proba played her part in bringing the gold and silver of pagan diction out of Egyptian bondage.

The influence of Christian theory on Christian Latin poetry is suggested by the preoccupation of the poets with the problems of assimilating pagan poetic diction. It may be argued that further illustration of Latin practice will not be useful for our study of Christian poetry in English. On the other hand, it is not possible to study directly the English poets' adaptation of pagan diction to Christian purposes because texts written in the Germanic vernacular before the advent of Christianity do not survive. Furthermore, surviving early treatises on rhetoric or on metrics were written in Latin and were concerned with the writing of Latin, the enduring language of literature. The vernacular, whatever the acclaim accorded its success, was the language of ephemera. Its transcription was probably in those early days a matter of the chance interest of bishop or abbot; certainly its survival has been a matter of chance. Since there are no early theoretical writings on vernacular composition, but only on composition in Latin, and since the survival of vernacular literature is largely the result of the interest of men who were trained in Latin rhetoric and Latin poetry, we must of necessity study English poetry in the light of the practice of Latin poetry.

Fortunately a point of connection between Latin and English poetry exists in the work of the two great monastic writers, Aldhelm and Bede, both of whom wrote English as well as Latin poems. Their recorded practice of writing in English may well have stemmed from the Irish influence on English Christian culture, for the Irish tended to retain their own language as the basic mode of oral and written expression.[9] The primacy of Latin in the writings of Aldhelm and Bede resulted from the preponderance of the Roman influence, which encouraged the use in serious writing of Latin rather than the native vernacular. But Irish and Roman monks did not differ in their agreement on essential Augustinian principles. As Roger has pointed out, the Irish and English churches together succeeded in realizing *"the plan traced by St. Augustine."* [10] Since the English Church inherited Augustine's program of Christian culture, we may study the poetry of Aldhelm and Bede in the light of Augustinian theory.

Aldhelm

Aldhelm, who became an abbot and then a bishop among the West Saxons, received his first training from an Irish monk, Maeldubh; subsequently he studied at Canterbury under Theodore and Hadrian, monastic emissaries of the Roman Pope. Thus in Aldhelm the two influences, Irish and Roman, first integrate and coalesce. Moreover, Aldhelm, according to William of Malmesbury, composed English verses to attract listeners to his serious words: he "gently, led back the citizens to health by interweaving among the foolish things, the words of Scripture." [11] That is, Aldhelm gave his popular fictions a Christian significance, a practice which illustrates Roger's statement that the English Church, "far from forbidding the popular songs, so widespread among the Saxons, made use of them to further Christian doctrine." [12]

Aldhelm wrote extensively in Latin, and, unlike his work in English, a considerable body of this Latin writing in verse and prose survives. In these writings Aldhelm shows the impress of the Augustinian tradition: (1) in his concern with the problem of Christianizing pagan vocabulary and (2) in his conception of the function of poetry.

His Latin verse abounds in Christianized pagan epithets. Olympus stands frequently for Heaven, Tartarus for Hell; God is frequently called the King of Olympus. But more than this, his Christian use of the language of pagan myth is frequently complex. In the beginning of the *De virgine,* after a prayer to God, he specifically disclaims the inspiration of the Muses:

> I do not seek the *rustic Muses* for my verses and periods, nor do I seek for my metrical songs the *Castalian nymphs,* the service of whom the *Heliconians* called a celestial yoke; nor do I pray that *Phoebus* grant a fluent tongue in speech—he whom *Latona creatrix* produced on Delos: I do not deign to speak in abominable verses as once the melodious poet is said to have spoken; "Helicon goddesses, lay open and instruct my song." But rather I strive to move the Thunderer with my prayers, Who grants to use the oracles of peaceful word; I seek the word from the *Word,* Whom the psalmist sang, born in the heart of the Father, Who remained the Only-Begotten, through Whom the Omnipotent Father created everything throughout the world; so the Cherishing Spirit of the Father and the Son deign to give aid clemently to his unworthy servant.[13]

Aldhelm here does not deny indiscriminately the validity of pagan sources of inspiration; rather, as his choice of epithets and his pattern of contrasts suggest, he concedes some measure of truth to pagan fictions, while denying them a full measure of truth. Thus Apollo, the son of *Latona creatrix,* is contrasted with the Word, the son of God. As in the *Phoenix,* Phoebus Apollo allegorically represents Wisdom, Christ—but only for the Christian who perceives the truth behind the parable, the real behind the appearance.[14] Considered literally, as a god of the sun, Apollo reveals the ignorance of pagan worship and the superficiality of pagan poetic inspiration. Similarly the pagan poetic fiction that represented the fountain of Helicon as the source of poetic inspiration contained a profound truth at which the pagan in parable blindly guessed; the Christian truth reveals that the only fountain of inspiration is the Well of Life, again an epithet for Christ. Further, the Mount of Helicon represents the Mount of Sion, the true heavenly source of inspiration. God is called by Aldhelm the Thunderer, an epithet for Jupiter in pagan poetry. The Father, described in the Old Testament as speaking in the thunder, is represented in the pagan myths by the figure of Jupiter. Aldhelm, in short, suggests by his complex figure that the pagan letter (or flesh, or rind, or shell) is given life by the Christian spiritual truth (soul or kernel) which is hidden in it.

The same subtle handling of the representational values of pagan myth is illustrated in Riddle 79, *The Sun and the Moon:*

> Jupiter, most wicked son of Saturn, whom the songs of the poets call mighty, did not give us birth, nor was our mother on Delos, Latona creatrix; I am not Cynthia, my brother is not Apollo. No, the Governor of highest Olympus gave us birth, Who now reigns over the high arch of heaven.[15]

Aldhelm contrasts Jupiter, the son of Saturn, not, as we might expect, with the God of Sinai, but with the Ruler of Olympus! The explanation is that he is playing on the contrast between the literal significance of Jupiter, a creature of man's fancy, and the anagogical value of Jupiter as God, the Creator: the one was made in time, the Other is eternal. In Riddle 7, *Fate*, Aldhelm

71

treats of the difference that Christian revelation has made for the idea of fate:

> It is known that once the eloquent poet sang, "Where God and harsh Fortune call, let us follow." Falsely the Ancients were accustomed to call me Mistress, ruling with the sceptre of the world until the Grace of Christ may rule.[16]

The Christian sees in Fortune the agent of God's Providence: Fate, the mistress of the world, is not ruler, but regent.

Aldhelm's concern with Christianizing the language of pagan myth is merely part of his total religious attitude toward poetry. His high seriousness is not belied by his occasional use of acrostics [17] or by his occasional—perhaps not very serious—venture into the Hesperic style: "Primitus pantorum procerum praetorumque pio potissimum paternoque praesertim privilegio panegericum poemateque passim prosatori. . . ." [18] Nor is his seriousness compromised by his writing of riddles, because as he says in his preface, his "rude" verses are made in thanks to God, "Sic, Deus, indignis tua gratis dona rependis." [19] The statement itself is expressed so enigmatically as to defy obvious translation: "Thus, Lord, for unworthy thanks Thou repayst thy gifts." What Aldhelm means by repaying of gifts for thanks becomes clear only when we supply what he leaves unstated: To praise God worthily one must, in fact, be given the gift of grace, but this gift of grace is itself so great that it makes unworthy the expression of thanks. Aldhelm's verses, which are intended to give God the thanks of praise, need a further gift from God, grace, which in turn exceeds all gratitude.

Aldhelm specifically disavows a secular purpose in the riddles.[20] He will not, he says, "summon Castalian nymphs"; he will not "lie down and dream dreams on Parnassus"; God alone, "the Creator, Patron of poets," must be the inspiration for his verses, for "if He touches man's heart, forthwith it sings out in praise: as did Moses and the psalmist who prophesied the Redeemer." Because he is writing for the glory of God he must write as well as he can, since nothing done for the glory of God should be done unworthily, but the writing of riddles is not thereby justified. Aldhelm's actual purpose in writing riddles is suggested by the fact that they are part of a treatise chiefly devoted to metrics. The riddles serve as an instructional interlude; their function is to provide mental exercise, what Marrou, speaking of Augustine, has called *gymnastique intellectuelle.* In short, Aldhelm proclaims the pre-eminence of the Bible without denying the utility of human letters which seek their inspiration from the God who inspired the Bible. The riddles have some resemblance to Scripture in that they seek to direct the mind toward the perception that words and created things veil underlying truths. Aldhelm, England's first literary figure of international repute, unmistakably takes his place in the Augustinian tradition.[21]

According to William of Malmesbury, as has been noted, Aldhelm composed songs in English. Thus with Aldhelm the Augustinian tradition of Christian Latin poetry meets the beginnings of Christian literature in English. Unfortunately, although his influence upon the spread and development of poetry in English must have

73

been great, no surviving English poem may be attributed directly to Aldhelm. But a curious verse fragment in eulogy of him, written perhaps by one of his students, helps to suggest one of the ways in which Aldhelm's interest in the enigmatic style helped to influence vernacular practice; and his riddle *Lorica* (cuirass) was translated very early into Old English—and so excellently that it has been suggested the translation may well be Aldhelm's own.[22] Since there are no others, these two pieces, the fragment and the riddle, must suffice to suggest the result of Aldhelm's influence upon English vernacular poetry.

The fragmentary eulogy of Aldhelm is macronic (Greek, Latin, and English). It begins with the book imagined as speaking:

þus me gesette *sanctus et iustus* — Thus he composed me holy and righteous

beorn boca gleaw *bonus auctor* — man wise in books the good author

Ealdhelm æþele sceop *etiam fuit* — Aldhelm, noble poet, also was

ipselos on æþel Angelsexna — eminent in his native land of the Anglo-Saxons

byscop on Bretene. *Biblos* ic nu sceal . . . — bishop in Britain. A book I now shall . . .[23]

The tribute, with its riddling quality, would not have displeased the master. For Aldhelm, like Augustine himself, would have felt no conflict in employing wordplay for serious purposes. What seems trivial to us seemed then a sign of literary competence, promoting a better and more vigorous grasp of underlying meaning. The wordplay in the poem, on *æþele* (noble) and *æþel* (native land), fulfills the requirements of wordplay in Christian theory, because it suggests an important underlying truth: Aldhelm is the *æþele sceop,* noble poet, or poet in his native land, that is, heaven, who is thus honored *in æþel,* that is, in the land of his birth, England.

Of Aldhelm's own writing in English, the OE version of his Latin riddle *Lorica* (cuirass) must serve in lieu of any surviving poem incontestably his. A literal English translation of this version of the riddle follows:

> Me the wet earth wondrously cold
> from its womb first gave birth:
> I know I am not made of fleeces of wool,
> of hair through great skill—as I think.
> Twisted woofs are not mine, nor have I warp,
> nor through me in rush of troops does thread roar,
> nor resounding shuttles shake me,
> nor from anywhere shall reeds strike me.
> Worms have not woven me through skill of fate,
> those who splendidly adorn the good yellow cloth;
> nevertheless, men will, widely over earth,
> call me a joyful robe for warriors.
> Nor do I fear the flight of arrows in dread of peril
> though they be taken eagerly from the quiver.[24]

What is of chief interest in the riddle is its evidence of structural and linguistic subtlety. It serves well to illustrate the close attention to detail which characterizes early Christian poetry in English and to illustrate the demands for active comprehension made upon the audience who heard such poems.

Structurally, the riddle is based on the juxtaposition of at-first-startling opposites. The poet develops the verbal

75

ambiguity that a breastplate is a coat yet is not made of wool or silk. He does this not simply to give a clue, by opposites, to the material of the breastplate, for it should be remembered that answers to the Latin riddles are given in the titles. Rather he wishes to emphasize the contrast between the imperviousness of the armor, and the wool, which in its manufacture is wounded by thread and shuttle—no arrow may wound the *lorica*. The imperviousness of the armor is contrasted to the silk, woven by worms. The breastplate is a more joyful robe than is "the web of worms" because it keeps a man from death. This idea is pointed up in the English version of the riddle, which defines the skill of the worms as a "skill of Fate." The silkworm obeys blindly the same fatal law to which all worldly finery is subject.

The selection of images in the riddle and its structure of implied contrast have the purpose of arousing the reader to perceive the hidden relationships that exist in the contrast between the iron in the earth and the iron which has realized the function of protecting man's life. This subtlety of purpose, obviously much different from that of a mere puzzle, is further illustrated by the linguistic dexterity of the poem. For example, if we turn to the *Etymologiae* of Isidore of Seville we discover a hint for the verbal structure of the riddle in the very etymology of the word *lorica:* "it is so-called in that it is lacking in thongs (*loris careat*) for it is covered with iron chains alone." [25] The contrast in the riddle between the cloth and the iron suggests the etymology of the word that is the answer to the riddle. Aldhelm perhaps intends us to perceive the mysterious fitness of word and thing, which testified to him of the divine inspiration of all created things.

Finally, a moral significance may be suggested in the consideration that although the *lorica* can keep man safe from arrows, nothing can keep him from eventual physical death. Man's real need is for a *lorica* of the soul, a more joyful garment for a man in peril than the breastplate, as the breastplate is more joyful than a web of worms. It is not unlikely that the spiritual implication of the *lorica* is intended by Aldhelm, since the image of the spiritual *lorica* is commonplace.[26] For example, in a hymn attributed to Columba, *In Te Christe,* Christ is called *lorica*.[27] The concept of the spiritual breastplate is to be found in the Hesperic Latin *Lorica,* attributed to Gildas.[28] St. Patrick's *Lorica,* according to its prose preface, is "a *lorica* of faith for the protection of body and soul against demons and men and vices." [29] The preface to the *Lorica* of Gildas promises that "on whatever day one will have said this prayer, men or demons, and enemies may not harm him, and death on that day does not touch him." Thus Aldhelm's riddle, *Lorica,* perhaps invites the perception that only the *lorica* of prayer will protect man against the arrows of temptation. In the context of Aldhelm's avowed purpose in writing, and in the context of the conventional use of *lorica* as a spiritual symbol, the riddle seems to belong to the tradition of Christian poetry and theory.

Doctrine and Poetry

Bede

Bede was a master of Latin learning and composed Latin poems, but in addition, according to the testimony of Cuthbert, a brother of Bede's own monastic house, Bede was thoroughly versed in traditional English songs (*doctus in nostris carminibus*) and composed songs in English. One of these survives because Cuthbert saw fit to transcribe it in his account of Bede.[30] It is called Bede's *Death Song* because Bede is said to have composed it shortly before his death:

> In the face of death's sudden danger no man becomes
> wiser in his thoughts than is his need
> for pondering before his going hence
> what to his spirit of good or of evil
> after death-day will be judged.[31]

The poem, spare and simple as it is, calls for analysis. Three key incremental phrases support its structure: (1) "in the face of death's sudden danger," (2) "before his going hence," (3) "after death-day." They provide a subtle interweaving of motifs. The first and third phrases are generalized absolutes, placed in apposition: death as threat—death as completed act. The second phrase is specific, *his* going hence, and is mediate in time between the two absolutes of death's beginning and death's completion: *before* death man faces *death's onslaught; going hence* man passes through death to eternity *after* death. Ideationally, the second phrase links the first and third phrases: the absolute, death's onslaught, should suggest to man that *before* death he live in preparation for the absolute of *after* death. This repetitive pattern gives to the poem its slightly enigmatic quality, a quality which appears in the attempt at literal translation. The effect of the slight ambiguity is to suggest more than is explicitly stated: that the true meaning of man's life is as a preparation for death.

Attention to the structure of the *Death Song* fixes in the mind of the reader the contrast between becoming and being, between the goal, which is after death, and the way to the goal, which is before death. The structure of the poem, despite its simplicity, has the virtue of compelling thoughtful consideration of the Christian doctrine that man's life is a pilgrimage from becoming to being. His wisdom is to understand that the good and evil he does before death will determine his being in eternity. He has no time for any other wisdom.[32]

Taken by itself, without reference to these Christian implications, the poetic structure of the *Death Song*, with its allusive parallels, seems fortuitous or merely conventional. But by observing how the structure of the poem suggests Christian truths we perceive that the song, though generalized in expression, implies a deeply felt and personal renunciation of human learning. What would be on the emotional surface of a modern poem is with Bede part of the general truth of holy living and holy dying. Only so far as the conduct of his own scholarly life may add poignancy and force to the moral truth in which Bede believed does it have any part in his *Death Song*.

The theme of the *Death Song* is developed at length in a Latin poem sometimes attributed to Bede, the *De die judicii*.[33] This judgment day poem is worth some attention here, not only because it helps to place the *Death Song* in perspective, but also because in the introductory lines highly developed use is made of biblical symbolism, a symbolism absent almost entirely from the straightforward, direct *Death Song*. The *De die judicii* has the further advantage for us that it was later translated into OE verse, so that we have an objective test of the limits of the understanding of symbolic subtleties on the part of the English translator and his audience. Briefly, the *De die judicii* pictures the speaker as sitting alone and dejected under a shade-bearing tree in a flowery place. Disturbed by a sudden sorrow, he begins to sing verses recalling his sins, death, Judgment, and the ensuing eternal punishments and rewards. From this introduction, the poet proceeds to the substance of his poem, which consists in an elaboration of the points outlined, developed through a fictitious monologue in which the speaker first addresses the veins of the body, imploring them to shed tears of repentance (12-32); then his mind, imploring it to seek its cure while there is still time (33-86); and finally his body, entreating it to think on what will happen to it on Judgment Day and contrasting the punishment of the damned with the joys of the blessed (87-157). The admonitory theme of repentance is clearly the same as that contained in the *Death Song*, and the dramatic form is itself interesting in its suggestion of internal dialogue between the soul and the body;

but what is of chief interest here is the introductory description (1-11), which may be explained as a symbolic statement of the theme of the entire poem. The poem begins:

Amidst the flowery grasses of the fertile earth,
with the blast of the winds everywhere in echoing branches,
under the cover of the shade-bearing tree, alone and dejected,
while I sat disturbed by a sudden bitter complaint,
I sang these wretched verses because of my sad mind,
as remembering the offences of my sins,
the stains of life and the hateful time of death,
in terrifying consideration of the Day of Judgment:
the eternal anger of the Strict Judge against the accused,
and all the race of men in their separate places:
the joys of the saints and the punishments of the damned.[34]

A literal interpretation of the opening lines of description (1-5) suggests that they have little to do, except by way of literary flourish, with the hortative theme of the poem, expressed compactly in lines 6-11. But such rhetorical display runs counter not only to the somberness of the remainder of the poem, but also to the high seriousness incumbent on the Christian poet in introducing a serious subject. Literary description for its own sake—mere rhetoric—is antithetical to the true purpose of Christian poetry. A pretty shell, rattling in emptiness, it falls under the ban of the Augustinian analysis of the verses of Claudian.[35] But if the initial description is read for its symbolic import, the contradiction disappears and the meaning of the opening lines may be shown to summarize the theme of the poem.

This symbolic or underlying meaning—the pearl in

the oyster—will be found in the Bible, specifically in the leading drama of the Fall of Man. In Genesis 3:8-10 Adam and Eve, after their sin, hide from the Lord under the tree in the garden:

> And they heard the voice of the Lord God walking in the garden in the breeze of the evening: and Adam and his wife hid themselves from the presence of the Lord God amidst the tree of the garden.
> And the Lord God called unto Adam, and said unto him, where art thou?
> And he said, I heard Thy voice in the garden, and I was afraid because I was naked: and I hid myself.[36]

Here is a central biblical referent for the flowery field (garden), the shadows of the tree, the wind, and even the sudden terror that fell upon the speaker in the poem.

Among the works doubtfully ascribed to Bede in Migne's *Patrologia* is a dialogue between master and disciple entitled *Quaestiones super Genesim*. The master explains certain symbolic truths about the incident of God walking in the garden. When man's heart is invaded by sin, he says, God leaves his heart. That is one meaning of God's walking in the garden in the breeze of evening:

> What is the meaning of the breeze of evening except that the more fervent light of truth has left, and the coldness of its guilt grips the sinful soul. For in the evening breeze, the first man after his sin is found hidden: because he has lost the midday heat of charity, now he lies stupefied in the shadows of sin as in the cold of the breeze, just as it is written concerning the same sinning man, *Because he has followed the shadow.* He has lost the heat of charity and has abandoned the sun and hidden himself within the shadows of his inner cold.[37]

82

The tree under which Adam seeks to hide, as Augustine explains, is the tree of the knowledge of good and evil, of whose forbidden fruit Adam has eaten.[38] This tree, which God placed in the middle of the garden, is not an evil tree except as man misuses it. Only because of man's corruption of this gift through disobedience does the tree become the symbol of man turned from God in self-love, of the man who has lost the heat of charity and seeks vain comfort in the world.[39] The result for man in hiding is dejection of spirit; for, as Augustine says, "When God turns away His inward countenance, man becomes distressed." [40] But God calls to Adam to signify His mercy; He calls distressful man "to penance." [41] The commentary, in generalizing the moral implications of the drama of the Fall, gives to the symbols of the garden a universal applicability: the symbol of a man sitting alone and dejected under the shade of a tree the leaves of which are blown by the wind represents one who is in the world and has been corrupted by its temptations so that he is cut off from God. If he awakens to some inner or outer voice of complaint, he symbolically awakens to the voice of God in his conscience recalling him to the memory of his heavenly home.

Between the independent use of these symbols in poetry and their use in a direct biblical connection, an intermediate stage is to be found, as for example in the *Alethias* of Claudius Victor, a "biblical epic" in Latin based on Genesis. In this poem we find the underlying meaning of biblical incident brought to the fore. In dealing with the actions of Adam and Eve after the first sin,

Claudius Victor in Book I sets forth the symbolic interpretation that we have just developed:

Adam and Eve desired, if perchance they might,
to hide themselves in the earth: thus neighbor to its punishment
is sin, so that now these wretched ones, mortally fearful,
the image of death makes rejoice; woods and shaded sloughs
they spread over them, the deceiving comforts of a vain retreat.

.   .   .   .   .

But the Father's
sacred Mercy forbids despair, Whose clemency . . .
exceeds justice. For not with harsh voice
condemning where you are, what in trembling voice you ponder,
does He terrify, but rather He restores.[42]

The Christian poet translates the terms of the biblical incident immediately into the moral generalizations drawn from it by the Fathers. The wooded shade signifies man's vain recourse to worldly pleasure in order to hide his spiritual wretchedness. The voice is a voice calling to repentance.[43]

The vast exegetical work of the Fathers was constantly tending to extend and develop the range of biblical symbol. This knowledge did not remain the esoteric possession of the learned but was disseminated everywhere in Christendom through sermons. In the central labor of extending the symbolic import of words of the Bible and the things of God's creation, no document is more important than the *Moralia* of Gregory the Great. In the *Moralia* the descriptive terms of the opening lines of the *De die judicii* are employed for their independent symbolic significance, without reference to their ultimate source in the biblical account of the Fall. Thus flowers

(amid which the speaker of *De die judicii* sits) have for
Gregory a symbolic import relevant to man:

> *The world just as it is filled briefly with withering flowers, so
> with men.* For just as the flower, man comes forth that he may
> shine in the flesh; but he wastes away that he may be re-
> turned as putrefaction. For what are men born on earth unless
> flowers in a field. Bend the eyes of our heart over the extent
> of this present world, and lo! it is full of flowers as of men.
> Life therefore in the flesh is flower in its withering.[44]

The flowers that surround the speaker in the poem pro-
vide a reminder of his mortality, and of the folly of de-
light in the world. Leaves blown by the wind are also
given by Gregory a general value symbolic of fallen man-
kind: "What is man who fell in Paradise from the tree
but a leaf? What but a leaf, seized by the wind of temp-
tation and blown by the winds of desire?" [45] Moreover,
for Gregory, as for the writer of *De die judicii*, the wind
serves as a symbolic reminder of final things: on the one
hand, it signifies "the entire temptation of the ancient
enemy, which acts in the mind"; on the other hand, "the
warmth of spirit, which occupies the faithful mind."
These are, respectively, the north and south winds. The
violent north wind suggests the Last Days, "because in
the end of time the evil spirit will weightily occupy, with
the cold of his stupor, the minds of men." [46]

The poet who wrote the *De die judicii* wrote in Latin,
for clerks who were well versed in the background of
symbolic meaning. The details of the initial description
would have led such an audience directly to recall the
basic symbolism of the Fall, a symbolism nourished and

developed by all the Fathers and flowering in Gregory's use of symbol as explanatory fact. The shadow-bearing tree, the leaves blown by the wind, the grassy flowers, and the solitary human figure of the desolate speaker, all suggest to the mind accustomed to think in terms of biblical symbol a picture of man lost in the world, tempted, cut off from the love of God, sorrowful in his exile from the light and warmth of charity. His fearful awakening represents the voice of God, calling him in his conscience to think of final things, of eternal reward and punishment. The significance of the description depends entirely on symbolic interpretation; the beauty of the description derives from its economy in setting forth symbolic meaning.

Since the *De die judicii* requires from its audience some understanding of biblical symbolism, the fact that it was translated into OE verse presents a problem of great significance for our understanding of the relation between Latin Christian and English Christian poetry. Although the translation—in the surviving version, at least—is much later than the Latin original, the modifications in the English poem have pertinence in suggesting what the translator found necessary to explain in order to make the poem understandable to an audience ignorant of Latin and thus without the specialized training presupposed by the original poet. The version in OE represents an expansion of the original but remains faithful to it, so that it should be possible to discover whether the translator was aware of, and felt that he could convey, the symbolic import of the opening lines. If he can be shown to have understood and attempted to convey symbolic meaning, a direct line of transition between Christian verse in Latin and in English may be shown to exist. It also follows that the audience for which the vernacular literature was written had some grasp of Christian symbolism.

Be Domes Dæge, as the English version of *De die judicii* is called, begins thus (in modern English):

> Lo I sat alone within a grove
> covered with the shadow within the tree
> where fountains of water flowed and ran
> in the middle of an enclosed space—all just as I say,—
> Also there the joyful flowers waxed and bloomed
> here and there in that wondrous field,
> and the trees of the grove stirred and whispered;
> through terror of the wind, the sky was agitated
> and my wretched spirit was greatly troubled.
> Then suddenly, terrified and depressed, I
> raised in song these saddened verses—
> all just as you said—I remembered my sins,
> the evils of life and the long time
> of the dark coming of death on earth.
> I dreaded also the great judgment
> for my evil deeds on earth;
> and also that eternal anger I dreaded
> and each sinful act before God Himself
> and how the mighty Lord all mankind
> would separate and judge through his secret might.
> I remembered this in myself and I mourned greatly
> and mourning I spoke in my heart oppressed.[47]

Only the details of the introductory description need be of concern in comparing the Latin and English poems. The English translator has added to the details in the original. The tree of the Latin poem is placed *within a grove, in the midst of an enclosure.* This grove the English poet fills with fountains about which the Latin poem is silent, except for the suggestion that the field is fertile. The *De die judicii* is silent also about the agitation of the sky, prominently featured in the English version. Furthermore, the striking beginning of the Latin poem, *Inter florigeras* (amid flowers), is not translated by the English poet until line 5 of his version. This transposition takes on significance in the light of the rubric which ends the English poem in the manuscript: "Here ends this book which is called *inter florigeras,* that is, in English, among the blossoming who go to God's Kingdom and how those suffer who go to hell." The rubricator seems to understand the symbolic import of the opening phrase of the poem (which poem, it should be noted, he attributes to Bede): the flowers signify for him men on earth, going to eternal reward or punishment, and he names the poem on the basis of this key initial phrase.[48]

In view of the obvious importance of the opening phrase, it would seem that the English poet must either have been ignorant of its symbolic value or have had some purpose in giving initial emphasis, not to the image of the flowers, but to the loneliness of the speaker in the grove. ("Lo! I sat alone.") His purpose stems from the fact that the Latin original was written for an audience with Latin learning—that is, an audience of clerics —and the English version for an audience without Latin learning. Bede, without hesitation, could rely on his audience to understand the significance of flowers, the tree, and the wind. Clerics who had themselves read Gregory and Augustine needed no clues beyond the bare descriptive facts to enable them to arrive at the correct underlying meaning. But the English poet could not rely on this economy of symbol to convey the desired meaning. His audience knew the exegetical writings of Bede, Gregory, Augustine, only at second hand through English homilies. Because they needed additional clues, additional signposts, to suggest what the trained cleric knew automatically, the English poet had to enforce and drive home the meaning of the symbolic description. At the same time, he had to maintain the symbolic quality of the introductory lines; to have given their underlying meaning outright would have defeated their purpose as intellectual exercise.

The English poet found it necessary to indicate at the outset that the speaker in the poem was alone, because this information gave his hearers a basic clue to the meaning of the ensuing symbols; they could apparently be relied on to know what would have been driven home to them in every church, that a man is truly alone only when he is cut off from the Christian community which lives in the love of God and the love of neighbor because of God. The symbol of the lonely man, sitting in the shadows, was apparently without the ambiguity of meaning involved in the symbol of the flowery field, which may signify both the world and Paradise. The learned audience could be relied upon to keep the two meanings in suspension until the relevance of the symbol was made clear by the introduction of the symbol of the dejected

man sitting under the shadows of a tree. For the un-
learned audience, it was clearly better to begin with a
symbol the relevance of which to the underlying mean-
ing of Genesis 3:8 is unambiguous.

Adam and Eve in the Vulgate Bible are said to "hide
amid a tree of Paradise," the tree of the knowledge of
good and evil. Their hiding under this particular tree is
symbolic of the fact that they have fallen into the error
of loving God's creation rather than the Creator. In hid-
ing under the tree of the knowledge of good and evil,
"which was in the middle of Paradise, they hide, that is,
in themselves, who were ordained to be in the middle
of things, below God and above the corporal." They
are "overwhelmed with wretched errors, the light of
truth having left them." [49] The mere mention of a shade-
giving tree in the particular context of the Latin poem
on Judgment Day was apparently sufficient to indicate
to the clerical audience what biblical symbol was in-
tended. But the English poet could not be certain that
his audience would be capable of such exactness of
reference; he had to offer some direction. In effect, he
directs his audience by beginning with the speaker sit-
ting *alone* under a tree *in a grove* (*innan bearwe*), so
as to delimit the possible references for the tree. This
is a tree within a grove, that is, a tree like that in the
middle of Paradise, which is described in the OE *Genesis*
poem as a tree in a grove, *beam on bearwe*. [50] The tree
is further identified with the tree in the middle of Para-
dise by the phrase in line 4 that is added in the English
poem, *on middan gehæge* (in the midst of an enclosure),

that is, a garden, Paradise, the *hortus deliciarum* in the midst of which stands the tree of knowledge of good and evil, under which Adam and Eve hid in the spiritual distress and loneliness occasioned by their sin.[51] To make doubly sure of the delimitation of reference to the tree "amid" which Adam and Eve hid, in *medio lignis paradisi*, the poet gives in line 2 a fairly close translation of the phrase, as he understood it, *holte tomiddes* (amid the tree). Finally, the grove or garden of the English poem is pictured as being watered, like Paradise, by streams which run through it (Gen. 2:10).[52] Thus the shade-bearing, wind-troubled tree and the well-watered garden surrounding it are details of description derived from the biblical Garden of Eden, and they serve not only to give emphasis but also to enlarge the scope of his audience's interpretive understanding.

Of further pertinence is the poet's development of the dejection of the speaker. As in the Latin poem, the speaker hears the wind in the branches, but now in a developed symbolic context:

> And the trees of the grove stirred and whispered,
> through terror of the wind, the sky was agitated
> and my wretched spirit was greatly troubled.

The English poet has added the detail of the agitation of the sky, which he connects directly with the speaker's agitation; and in the phrase, "through terror of the wind," he employs the device of double reference. The trees of the grove are stirred through terror of the wind, but similarly stirred are the sky and the speaker's own wretched spirit; the phrase looks both forward and backward. The result is, of course, to link the meaning of the symbolic details; both the disturbance in the trees and the disturbance of the sky are connected with the speaker's disturbance and reinforce its symbolic meaning. For example, the figurative disturbed sky appears often in Gregory, as in his comment on Job 30:15:

> *I am reduced to nothing. Like the wind You have taken away my delight. And like a cloud my security has passed away.* . . . The wind takes away delight, just as when a transitory object destroys the desire for eternity. . . . The cloud indeed stands prominent on high, but the wind blows it on that course.[53]

Evil is a denial of good, and evildoers are actually driven by a loss of their desire for eternity, so that evildoers who seem to reach the heights are in actuality "blown on the course of their daily life as if by the winds of mortality." Elsewhere, as in his commentary on Ezechiel 1:9, Gregory considers that the symbol of the sky with its clouds agitated by the wind represents the sinner "moved by the impulse of temptation." [54]

The English poet's addition of the symbolic detail of the wind-driven sky serves as an additional clue to the speaker's melancholy loneliness, suggesting that he is moved by the winds of temptation, an exile from the love of God; the addition serves also to connect the symbolic meanings of the wind in the leaves with the meaning of the speaker's plight: He too is a leaf and a cloud, blown by the wind of desire in the cold of the evening under the shadow of the evil tree of desire. From this state only the good wind of the voice of God may call him back—the voice of God in the garden of his mind. To emphasize the difference in the speaker's situation before and after he heeds the voice of God within him, the English poet has added two parenthetical and contrasting phrases, "all just as I say" (*eall swa ic secge* [4]) and "all as You said" (*eall swylce þu cwæde* [12]). When the speaker sits under the shade of the tree, he is, as Augustine says, hiding in himself.[55] Thus he speaks from himself—"all just as I say." But after he has heard the voice of God in the wind and has begun to raise his voice in penitential song, he is restored to God in charity. He speaks in accord with God—"all as You said." Finally, having heeded the voice, penitentially he begins by asking that his veins, the fountains of repentance within, weep for his sins:

> Now do I, oh veins, verily entreat
> that you truly open the wellsprings
> quickly into tears hot on my cheeks
> when I sinful strike mightily with my fist,
> beat my breast in the place of prayer
> and my bodily home lay on the earth
> and the earned evil all I make known.[56]

These transitional lines suggest another reason for the addition of the detail of the springs that water the garden. This detail serves to tighten symbolic reference and also to connect the initial description with the body of the poem.

Christian poets, whether they wrote in Latin or English, expected their audiences to possess, in varying degrees, a common tradition of doctrine and symbol. They seem also to have expected their audiences to make a considerable effort to understand the underlying meaning of a poem. The writing of poetry could be justified only on the basis of its contributing to the propagation of the Faith. Listening to poetry required the same justification. Whatever the personal judgment about the poetry discussed in this chapter, it cannot be dismissed merely as "simple." Although the historical difficulty of this poetry cannot be judged by the measure of modern difficulty in comprehension, since what was once automatic has now become laborious, the fact remains that the poetry seems to require considerable intellectual effort even of a reader well versed in the symbolic subtleties of biblical interpretation.

The problems and purposes of Christian poets were much the same, whether they wrote in Latin or in English. Since Christian poetry written in English would appear to be a part of the same tradition that produced Latin Christian poetry, it is necessary now to see whether the evidence of other English Christian practice supports the view that Christian poetry has as its prime purpose the elevation of the mind to the perception of underlying truth. We will begin with the first Christian poem in English, Caedmon's *Hymn.*

NOTES TO CHAPTER III

1. Cappuyns, *op. cit.*, pp. 46-47. For accounts of this Latin poetry see the works of Manitius, Raby, Moricca, cited above. The verse is collected in the MGH.
2. *Op. cit.*, p. 199.
3. See Ch. I, n. 22.
4. Ed. R. Ellis, in *CSEL*, XVI, 247-249.
5. *Opera*, ed. Helm, pp. 3-80.
6. Text with useful translation in O. Kuhnmuench, *Early Christian Latin Poets* (Chicago, 1929), pp. 52-63. The allegorical meaning becomes part of the OE poetic version of this poem. (See *Anglo-Saxon Poetic Records*, ed. G. Krapp and E. Dobbie [New York, 1931], III, 84-112; hereafter cited as *Records*.)
7. Kuhnmuench, *op. cit.*, pp. 55-63.
8. Ed. C. Schenkl, in *CSEL*, XVI, 568. See Manitius, *op. cit.*, pp. 123-130.
9. M. Laistner, *Thought and Letters in Western Europe, A.D. 500 to 900* (London, 1931), p. 108.
10. Roger, *op. cit.*, p. 318 (italics mine); see also pp. 277, 285, 384. For an excellent account of the difficulties between the Irish and Roman Churches in England see R. Hodgkins, *History of the Anglo-Saxons* (Oxford, 1935), I, 282-302.
11. *Gesta Pontificum Anglorum*, V, ed. N. Hamilton ("Rolls Series," LII; London, 1870), p. 336. For discussions of Aldhelm see Roger, *op. cit.*, pp. 134-141.
12. Roger, *op. cit.*, p. 277. Sometimes indulgence in vernacular poetry was felt to be dangerous. See Alcuin's warning in *Monumenta Alcuina*, ed. W. Wattenbach and E. Duemmler ("Bibliotheca Rerum Germanicum," VI; Berlin, 1873), p. 357. See also Gregory's remarks to a Gallic bishop, cited by Laistner, *op. cit.*, p. 80.
13. *Opera*, ed. R. Ehwald, *MGH*, A.A. 15 (Berlin, 1919), pp. 353-354.
14. A similar idea is to be found in Fulgentius' explanation of the spiritual meaning of the nine Muses. (See Helm, *op. cit.*, p. 25.)
15. Ehwald, *op. cit.*, pp. 133-134. The riddles have been translated

by J. Pitman, *The Riddles of Aldhelm* ("Yale Studies in English," LXVII; New Haven, 1925).

16. Ehwald, *op. cit.*, p. 101. The quotation is from the *Aeneid.*

17. *Ibid.*, pp. 97-99. The verse preface to the riddles is so composed that the first and last letters of each line are the same. If they are read down they spell out a sentence proclaiming Aldhelm as author. See also the Prologue to the metrical *De virgine.*

18. Ehwald, *op. cit.*, pp. 488 and 487 n. See Hodgkin, *op. cit.*, p. 324; Laistner, *op. cit.*, pp. 119-120.

19. Ehwald, *op. cit.*, p. 97.

20. *Ibid.*, pp. 97-98. Compare Alcuin's use of riddles in his *Disputatio, PL,* 101, 1099.

21. Ehwald, *op. cit.*, p. 508. See William of Malmesbury, *op. cit.*, pp. 347-348. See also Aldhelm's Epistle 8 in Ehwald, *op. cit.*, p. 500.

22. A. H. Smith, *Three Northumbrian Poems* (London, 1933), pp. 18-19.

23. Ehwald, *op. cit.*, pp. 219-220; *Records,* VI, 97-98.

24. Smith, *op. cit.*, pp. 44-46. The translation, as with all subsequent ones, is literal and is put in verse form for sake of reference, not for metrical reasons.

25. Lindsay, *op. cit.*, XVIII, xiii.

26. J. Bernard and R. Atkinson, *The Irish Liber Hymnorum* (London, 1898), I, 133-136.

27. *Ibid.*, p. 85. For a brief discussion of other *lorica* prayers, see II, 208-212 and 242-244.

28. *Ibid.*, I, 206-210. For discussion see Manitius, *op. cit.*, p. 159; Moricca, *op. cit.*, III, 1386; Hodgkin, *op. cit.*, I, 256 and 322-323.

29. Trans. Bernard and Atkinson, *op. cit.*, II, 49-51.

30. In C. Plummer's edition of Bede's *Historia ecclesiastica,* I, clx.

31. Smith, *op. cit.*, p. 42.

32. See Marrou, *op. cit.*, App. B, pp. 561-569, for discussion of Augustine's use of the key words *sapientia* and *scientia.* A distinction between the two concepts represented by the words is involved in the poem.

33. H. Löhe, ed., *Be Domes Dæge* ("Bonner Beitrage," 22; Bonn, 1907). See Manitius, *op. cit.*, p. 86.

34. Löhe, *op. cit.*, pp. 7-8:

Inter florigeras fecundi caespitis herbas
flamine ventorum resonantibus undique ramis

arboris umbriferae moestus sub tegmine solus
dum sedi, subito planctu turbatus amaro,
carmina prae tristi cecini haec lugubria mente,
utpote commemorans scelerum commissa meorum
et maculas vitae mortisque inamabile tempus
iudiciique diem horrendo examine magnum
perpetuamque reis districti iudicia iram
et genus humanum discretis sedibus omne
gaudia sanctorum necnon poenasque malorum.

35. See Ch. I, nn. 24, 26.
36. Gen. 3:8 in the Vulgate differs from the King James version in that it refers not to "trees" but to a "tree" (*in medio ligni*) and has the Lord walk in the breeze (*ad auram*), not the cool of the evening: "Et cum audissant vocem Domini Dei deambulantis in paradiso ad auram post meridiem, abscondit se Adam et uxor ejus a facie Domini Dei in medio ligni paradisi." Aelfric, *Heptateuch*, ed. S. J. Crawford (London, 1922), p. 89, translates the last phrase, *in medio ligni paradisi*, thus: "on middan ðam treowe neorxnawonges."
37. *PL*, 93, 280.
38. *De Genesis contra Manichaeos, PL*, 34, 208.
39. *Quaestiones super Genesim, PL*, 93, 268. When he eats of the fruit, man is disobedient and loses the heat of charity (280): "Charitatis enim calorem perdiderat, et verum solem homo desuerit, et sub umbra se interni frigoris abscondit." Erigena explains the traditional view brilliantly in the *De divisione naturae, PL*, 122, 327. (See Ch. II, n. 51.)
40. *De Genesi ad litteram*, 11, 44(23).
41. *Quaestiones super Genesim, PL*, 93, 280: "Adam, ubi es? Per hoc quod vocat, signum dat quia ad poenitentiam revocat per hoc quod requirit, aperte insinuat quia peccatores jure damnandos ignorat."
42. Ed. C. Schenkl, in *CSEL*, XVI, 380, ll. 443-447, 462-467.
43. Very pertinent is Augustine's account of the final act of his own conversion, in *Confessions*, VIII (12)28; tree, garden, and voice are all there.
44. *On Job*, 14:2, *PL*, 75, 983.
45. *On Job*, 13:25, *PL*, 75, 980. See also *On Job*, 14:7-10, *PL*, 75, 986.
46. *Homilies on Ezechiel*, on Ezek. 1:4, *Et vidi, et ecce ventus turbinis veniebat ab Aquilone, PL*, 76, 799.

Doctrine and Poetry

47. *Records,* VI, 58; Löhe, *op. cit.,* pp. 6-8, ll. 1-25.

48. *Records,* VI, pp. lxx-lxxi: "The text begins . . . with a heading in red, as follows: 'Incipit versus Bede presbiter [sic]. De die iudicii Inter florigeras fecundi cespites herbas flamine uentorum resonantibus undique ramis.' At the end of the poem is another rubric: 'Her endaðð þeos boc þe hatte inter florigeras. ðæt is on englisc betwyx blowende þe to godes rice faraðð. Ond hu ða þrowiaðð. þe to helle faraðð.'"

49. *De Genesis contra Manichaeos, PL,* 34, 208: "Quis se abscondit a conspectu Dei, nisi qui deserto ipso incipit jam amore erat in medio paradisi, id est ad seipsos, qui in medio rerum infra Deum et supra corpora ordinati erant. Ergo ad seipsos absconderunt se, ut conturbarentur miseris erroribus, relicto lumine veritatis, quod ipsi non erant."

50. Line 902, *Records,* I, 30. Eve is explaining to God why she ate the apple.

51. See Isidore's description (Lindsay, *op. cit.,* XIV, iii, 2). See D. W. Robertson, Jr., "The Doctrine of Charity in Medieval Literary Gardens," *Speculum,* XXVI (1951), 24-49.

52. See Gregory's commentary on the evil garden of Behemoth (*PL,* 76, 671-675).

53. *PL,* 76, 170.

54. *Ibid.,* 814.

55. See above, n. 49.

56. *Records,* VI, 58, ll. 26-32.

Chapter IV

CAEDMON'S *HYMN*

CAEDMON'S *Hymn* survives because Bede included
a Latin translation of it in his *Ecclesiastical History* (and
because an early scribe saw the value of including the
English original in his copy). The manner in which the
first Christian poem in English is preserved is fortunate
because the poem can be studied from an established
frame of reference, Bede's concept of the purpose and
function of poetry. Bede's reaction to the poem provides
a test of the applicability of Augustinian poetics to the
study of Christian poetry in English. He tells the story
of Caedmon's *Hymn* thus: [1]

> In the monastery of Abbess Hild was a brother [named
> Caedmon] specially marked and honored through divine grace
> for he did create songs of piety and faith. Whatever he learned
> of divine Scripture through scholars, in a brief space of time
> he adorned and brought forth in the poetic form of the Eng-
> lish tongue, well wrought and of the greatest sweetness and
> inspiration. And through his songs made for the people, the
> hearts of many men were enkindled to turn from the world

Doctrine and Poetry

toward the companionship of eternal life. Likewise many another in the English nation followed his lead in making songs firmly fixed in the faith, but none might equal him in this because not by means of men nor through any man had he learned the art of song, rather had he been divinely inspired and had received the art of verse through the grace of God. And for this reason he could never make idle or lying songs but only such as were appropriate to true faith and fitting for his faithful tongue to sing.

Now this man had remained in the secular state until he was advanced in age and had never learned any song. Thus often at the feast when there was adjudged an occasion for rejoicing and each in turn was to sing to the accompaniment of the harp, then as he saw the harp near his place, he arose for shame from the feast and went home to his house.

At a certain time when he had done this and had left the house of feasting, he went out to the cattle-barn, for that night was his to watch. When he had, at the proper time, laid his limbs to rest and slept, then in his sleep a man stood before him, hailed and greeted him and called him by name, "Caedmon, sing me something."

Then he replied and said, "I can sing nothing, and that is why I left the feast and came hither, because I knew nothing to sing."

Again he who was speaking with him spoke "Nevertheless you must sing for me."

Then he said, "What shall I sing?"

Said he, "Sing to me of the Creation."

When he had received this answer, then forthwith he proceeded to sing in praise of God the Creator, verses and words which he had never heard, the order of which is this:

Nu we sculan herian   heofonrices weard
metudes myhte   ond his modgeþanc
wurc wuldorfæder.   Swa he wundra gehwilc
ece drihten   ord astealde.
He ærest gesceop   ylda bearnum
heofon to hrofe   halig scyppend.

100

Caedmon's Hymn

Middangearde mancynnes weard
ece drihten æfter tida
firum on foldum frea ælmyhtig.

Now we should praise the Ward of heaven's kingdom:/ the Might of God and His Wisdom,/ the Work of the Glory-Father. So he of each wonder,/ the Eternal Lord, established the beginning./ He first created for the sons of men/ heaven as a roof, the Holy Creator./ The middle-earth the Ward of Mankind,/ the eternal Lord, thereafter adorned/ for men on earth, Almighty Joy./

Then he arose from his sleep, and all that he had sung sleeping he retained in his mind, and to these words he soon joined in the same meter many another song worthy through God.

Subsequently, according to Bede, Caedmon was brought to the abbess, and his miraculous gift of song was tested. Convinced by these tests, Hild had scholars teach him. What he learned he turned into songs, which, in turn, the scholars transcribed. He wrote poems based on Genesis, Exodus, and other books of the Old Testament and on Christ's ministry, Passion, and so forth. His purpose was "in all these writings," as Bede says, "to draw men away from the love of sin and evil deeds and to arouse them to an eagerness and love for good deeds."

What was important for Bede in this story, we may be sure, was the miracle that solemnized the birth of Christian poetry in English. Yet in telling the story Bede shows no overwhelming surprise at the strangeness of the event; he simply treats the story seriously, with reverence. He had ample precedent, of course, for the connection of poetry with religious inspiration. The word itself had been connected even by pagans with religious ceremonial in praise of their gods. More important for Bede, the Bible, the word of God, contained poetry that was by definition divinely inspired and was considered to be the first poetry written by men.[2] That God should specially mark with the honor of divine grace the first Christian poem in English must have seemed to Bede miraculous but, paradoxically, not surprising. Consequently he felt none of the doubts that today we feel and had no need to explain what in his account we now find difficult to understand. Nevertheless, for the students of literature the miraculous poem presents a special problem in critical judgment: Does the poem itself represent a worthy beginning to English poetry, or does its only worth rest in its historical position?[3]

First of all, Bede was probably not much concerned about anything but the miracle itself and its revelation of God's meaning. "His business was religion; even his interest in the actual poetry produced by the miracle is a religious one."[4] Another way of saying this is that his attitude toward poetry is Augustinian. Thus, without compromise of religious seriousness he responded to the beauty he perceived in the poem and testified to his inability to translate it since translation involves "loss of beauty and loftiness."[5] For Bede God, through his angel, was the true author of the *Hymn*. Since God is the source of all beauty, it follows that for Bede the *Hymn* had some relation to the divinely inspired poetry of Scripture. Angelic inspiration implies revelation: The angel brings to a chosen vessel, characteristically humble, the obligation to receive and to be the first to communicate God's word in English poetry. In consequence and within the limitations of its language, Caedmon's *Hymn* must for the believer have seemed as nearly perfect as man's work may be; either the poem was beautiful to the eyes of faith, or there was no miracle. It is impossible that God should have inspired what is inferior or merely workmanlike. Since the demands of faith on the little poem were very large, Bede must have seen in it much more than the best disposed modern is likely to allow. Hence the question: How could Bede have found in the brief and simple hymn an exemplification of true Christian poetry? In short, how would he have found in the *Hymn* that exercise of the mind which promotes understanding?

Since Caedmon sings of the creation and celebrates the might of God in establishing the beginning of created things, in particular of heaven and earth, his *Hymn* is to be related to the opening verses of the first chapter of Genesis: "In the beginning God created heaven and earth. . . ." But surely, even for Bede, there must have appeared something of an anticlimax if all that was involved in the angelic inspiration was the simple elaboration of the beginning of Genesis in the repetitive parallels of OE verse. An approach toward understanding what Bede saw in the *Hymn* is provided by biblical commentary on the opening verses of Genesis.[6] For the Fathers of the Church, as for the priest delivering a sermon to the people, the opening verses of Genesis had acquired dogmatic connotations. The verses did not stand alone. Their underlying meaning had become a basic and indispensable part of Christian doctrine.[7]

Bede himself wrote synoptic commentaries on Genesis.[8] As he points out, he relies chiefly on the authoritative hexameral commentary of Basil, as translated into Latin by Eustatius, on the commentary of Ambrose, and on that of Augustine. These commentaries, to which may be added that of Isidore, are basic and indispensable, and they, along with Bede's own commentary, should afford us some guide to the meaning that Genesis had for him.[9] We discover immediately that the opening verse of Genesis was considered especially to reveal the divine source of scriptural inspiration. The first verse of Genesis was said to have been written by Moses "in the spiritual excellence of revelation as if he were a witness of divine truth." Caedmon, too, was inspired, for according to Bede his *Hymn* was "a heavenly gift" (*caelestiem gratiam*) granted him by God. Genesis was said to be pure and without the worldly taint inherent in works written "in the conviction of human wisdom or in the pretenses and disputes of philosophy." [10] Caedmon's *Hymn* was written by a man so far from pretension to worldly learning that he even lacked the knowledge of song possessed by his unlettered fellows. To underscore the divine inspiration and purpose of Genesis, St. Basil calls Moses not the writer but "the *editor* of this scripture . . . Who, equal to the angels in having seen God, makes known to us what he heard from God." Thus the words of Moses, read in the light not of "human wisdom" but of spiritual doctrine, aided in "the salvation of those who learn." [11] Similarly, through Caedmon's "songs made for the people, the hearts of many men were enkindled to turn from the world toward the companionship of eternal life." And again, "Caedmon labored to remove men from the love of wickedness and to excite them truly to an eagerness and love of good deeds."

Comparison of the power of Caedmon's poem with the efficacy of the opening of Genesis provided Bede with a pragmatic test of the worth of the poem, although he did not, of course, believe that Moses and Caedmon were really comparable. Moses had seen God face to face and in this was the "equal of the angels"; whereas Caedmon was inspired to write in praise of God's creation in a vision and through the intervention of an angel. Yet a clear line of relationship connects Caedmon, the poet who wrote about Scripture in the vernacular, and Moses, who, in the language of Adam, wrote Scripture itself. Although Bede would have distinguished degrees of veneration to be accorded the word of God as reported by Moses and a divinely inspired poem, he would have expected each, in its degree, to contain some revelation and therefore to be worthy of the closest study.

For Bede the best evidence of the authenticity of Caedmon's vision would have been that the *Hymn* reflects some of the divine truths implanted by God through the agency of Moses in the beginning of Genesis. These truths—or some of them at least—had been brought to the knowledge of the faithful through the commentaries of the Fathers. Not only the verse, but also the very form, the order of words, *in principio fecit deus coelum et terram,* was considered by the Fathers to be divinely inspired and uniquely beautiful.[12] What literary criticism meant to the Christian of the early Middle Ages is suggested by St. Basil's delighted discovery that the very form of the first verse is itself meaningful: *"In principio fecit Deus,* Lo! the beauty of order in which Moses placed the beginning first," for thus Moses set forth the fundamental truth that God *created* the world, that it was not "engendered or innate." Immediately thereafter he set down the verb, *fecit,* Basil continues, to show "that the miracle of the creation is a little part of the excellence of the Maker." Then to teach man to "seek Who is the Maker, Moses, as if fixing a sign of his care, reverently introduced the name of God," *Deus.*[13] St. Ambrose also exclaims at "the excellent ordering" of placing *in principio* first, "so that Moses asserts that first which heretics were wont to deny." Ambrose finds even further artistic subtlety in the order of words, with *fecit* following *in principio:* "And beautifully Moses added *fecit* lest there be supposed a delay in creation." Furthermore, Moses in adding the subject, *Deus,* immediately after the verb, *fecit,* takes advantage of the natural human desire "to seek the Maker Who gave a beginning to so much work, Who so quickly made it." The result for Ambrose is absolute conviction: "You have heard the Author, you cannot doubt. . . . You can see because man did not discover this, rather God announced it."[14] St. Augustine eloquently agrees with Ambrose concerning the power of the opening verse of Genesis: "Marvelous the profundity of Thy words whose outer show is before us guiding the little ones. Terror there is in looking within, the terror of honor and the trembling of love." [15]

Although these judgments by men whose business was religion are basically religious, they are, nonetheless, aesthetic. As the *De doctrina* suggests, the Fathers were concerned with spiritual meaning, but they were concerned with the beautiful as well, with the placing of the best words in the best possible order. For them harmony and number are beautiful only because they reveal in outward formal symmetry the spiritual harmony and order of the Creator. [16] St. Basil and St. Augustine considered the first verse of Genesis to be beautiful because the form reveals an inner meaning consonant with spiritual truth. In its perfect fusion of form and meaning the verse serves as a model for the beautiful in Christian writing. Caedmon's creation hymn, to seem divinely inspired, must have appeared to reflect the supreme excellence of its source. Bede's "appreciation" of the *Hymn* would in turn have derived from a method of reading it similar to that which led to his appreciation of the biblical verses on the creation, except that in the *Hymn* he would seek not original revelation, but simply reaffirmation of biblical truths. It is against these truths that the arrangements of the parts of the *Hymn* must be balanced. Biblical commentary may provide a method for approaching the poem and a key to its order and meaning.

The *Hymn* falls naturally into three main divisions.

Doctrine and Poetry

The first two and one-half lines state the theme of praise:

> We should praise the Ward of Heaven:
> the Might of God, His Wisdom,
> the Glory-Father's Work.

There follows a general statement about God's creation:

> So He of each wonder
> the Eternal Lord established the beginning.

Finally comes the paraphrase of the first verse of Genesis:

> He first created for the sons of men
> heaven as a roof, the Holy Creator,
> then the middle-earth, the Ward of Mankind,
> Eternal Lord, thereafter adorned
> for men on earth, the Almighty Joy.

What might Bede have perceived in this arrangement?

The initial theme of praise he would have felt to be especially appropriate to a creation hymn. Ambrose considered that heaven and earth were created in the beginning "in evidence of things unseen," and he cites Psalm 18:1, "The heavens proclaim the glory of God and the firmament announces the works of His hands," to show that the function of the creation is to praise God.[17] Significantly, the theme of praise of the Creator by his creatures formed from the very earliest times the substance of the Preface in the Ordinary of the Mass: "Vere dignum et justum est, aequum et salutare, nos tibi semper et undique gratias agere, domine sancte, Pater omnipotens, aeterne Deus." This is the portion of the Mass, according to Walafrid Strabo, "in which the

will of the people is directed toward thanksgiving." [18]
Inspired by the words of the Preface and finding in them
an excellent introduction to his poem on Genesis, St.
Hilary of Arles begins his *In Genesim:*

> Dignum opus et iustum semper tibi dicere grates
> omnipotens mundi genitor, quo principio cuncta
> natalem sumpsere diem atque exorta repente
> post tenebras stupidi spectarunt lumina caeli.

> Worthy and right is it always to say thanks to You/ Almighty
> Creator of the world, in which Beginning all things/ assumed
> their natal day and, suddenly born/ after the shadows, amazed,
> looked at the lights of heaven.[19]

Caedmon in English is making the same connection of
ideas. The purpose of God's creation is to praise and
glorify His name. This purpose is especially revealed in
the creation itself. In beginning with the theme of praise,
Caedmon seems to give emphasis to what is most im-
portant for man to learn: that he should praise God in
word and works. Bede would certainly have perceived
the connection of ideas and would have appreciated
the opening theme of praise for its appropriateness to the
subject of the *Hymn,* the creation.

In his admonition to praise God, Caedmon develops
the reasons for praise of the Ward of Heaven in three
parallel epithets: "the Might of God," "His Wisdom,"
"the Glory-Father's Work." In these three epithets Bede
might well have found a trinitarian significance. The
belief in "God the Father Almighty, Creator of heaven
and earth," as triune was established by St. Athanasius
as the basic article of Christian faith. In this regard the

opening verses of Genesis were especially important be-
cause they represented for the Fathers the *locus classicus*
of scriptural evidence for the Trinity. Aelfric, much later
than Caedmon but in his language, gives succinctly the
conventional patristic interpretation:

> The Almighty Creator showed Himself through the great work
> which he created in the beginning, and He wished his creatures
> to perceive his glory and dwell with Him in glory eternally.
> . . . Here is the Holy Trinity in these three persons: the Al-
> mighty Father, born of no other, and the great Wisdom born
> of the Wise Father alone without beginning. . . . Now is the
> Love of Both ever the same with Them, that is the Holy Ghost,
> Who vivified all things.

Aelfric here summarizes the standard interpretation of
the beginning of Genesis, by which the verses are made
to reveal not only the Creator, but also the three elements
or parts of the act of creation. The three elements distin-
guished are aspects of the Creator, manifest in His act
of creation; and they represent the Three Persons in One
Creator. As Aelfric explains in one of his Catholic
homilies, the creation was accomplished through the
act of the Father, by the agency of Wisdom, the Son, and
completed in Love, or Will, the Holy Spirit.

How the Fathers arrived at this underlying meaning
is illustrated by Aelfric in his Preface to Genesis:

> *In the beginning God created the heaven and earth.* It is literal
> truth that God Almighty, as He wished, made in the begin-
> ning, created things. Nevertheless according to the spiritual
> understanding that beginning is Christ, just as He Himself
> said to the Jews, "I am the Beginning Who speak to you."
> Through this beginning God the Father wrought heaven and

earth, because He created all creation through the Son Who was eternally born of Him, the Wisdom of the Wise Father. Afterward, in the next verse in the book stands . . . *The Spirit of God brooded over the waters.* God's Spirit is the Holy Spirit through Whom the Father vivified all creation which He shaped through the Son.[20]

Aelfric is quoted not because the ideas he expressed are in any way original with him, but simply because he wrote in English and with masterful clarity. He is, of course, reiterating a patristic commonplace.[21] The Fathers ascribe "to the Father the creation of the world, to the Son, the disposition of things, to the Holy Spirit, the vivifying or ornamenting of all things." [22] In the representation of the Trinity through the creation, God the Father is the Power or Might, the Son is the Shaping Wisdom, the Holy Ghost, the Perfection of the Work.

These commonplaces of patristic interpretation might well have prepared Bede to perceive the mystery of the Trinity in the three aspects of God's creation singled out in the *Hymn* as demanding praise:

> metudes myhte   ond his modgeþanc,
> wurc wuldorfæder

The Might of God and His Wisdom [the thought of his mind],/ the Work of the Glory-Father.

The three phrases reflect the traditional division of the three Persons of the Trinity as they are revealed in Genesis: the Might of God, the Creator, would represent the Father; the Thought of the Father, His plan and disposition of creation, the Son; the Work, the Holy Ghost. Insofar as the opening lines seem to reflect in their

111

Doctrine and Poetry

ordering the eternal truth, that is, God, they also reflect the radiance of God, the only source of beauty. To discover, in the ordering of the words of the *Hymn,* the revealed truth was for Bede to perceive its formal beauty.

The first part of the *Hymn* consists in an exhortation to praise the Creator and possibly in an implicit suggestion of the mystery of the Trinity as revealed in the creation. In the second part of the poem Caedmon paraphrases "in the beginning":

> So He, of each wonder
> the Eternal Lord, established the beginning.

This beginning occurred, according to St. Basil, outside time, for "just as the beginning of the way is not the way, and the beginning of a house is not yet the house, thus also the beginning of time is not yet the fullness of time, nor even a small part of time." [23] "In the beginning" teaches us that God created outside of time in His eternity. He established the beginning of all from nothing (*ex nihilo*). Moreover, that act of creation in the beginning "gives the form of the future circles of the years." All that was to be in time was created in idea in the beginning.[24] This mystery of time and eternity, of which Augustine speaks at length in his commentary in the *Confessions,* is suggested in the second section of Caedmon's *Hymn* by the setting off of the adjective "eternal" against the noun, "beginning." The verses thus specifically describe, not the creation of all things, but the creation of their beginning.

Caedmon's Hymn

Patristic exegesis has more to reveal about the under-
lying meaning of "in the beginning." The creation in the
beginning was not of the heaven and earth "as man now
sees them." [25] The earth, we are informed immediately
in Genesis, was then *idle* and *empty*. But why should the
idle emptiness of the earth be introduced "without men-
tion of the heaven, except that nothing like this is to be
understood of that heaven; for this is the very higher
heaven which, secret from all condition of this revolving
world, remains always quiet in the glory of divine pre-
science." [26] The world, which exists in time, could not
yet exist in the beginning, which, timeless, gives the
form of time; therefore the heaven created in the begin-
ning must have been the eternal heaven, the *coelum
coeli,* of which God is Ward. [27] In contrast the earth is
yet formless. The eternal heaven was inhabited in the
beginning by spiritual beings, "not coeternal with the
Trinity, but participating in that eternity." [28] For simul-
taneously with the creation of the spiritual heaven, as
Bede says, "it was filled with the blessed troops of angels,
. . . called the sons of God to distinguish them, in truth,
from the saints, who were created later." [29] But, as St. Am-
brose points out, in another sense, the heaven created
in the beginning was created for man. For the spiritual
heaven was a model for the heaven that man sees as "the
highest of visible things." The temporal heaven, which
is "the ornament of the world," is also "the representation
of things invisible, the evidence of things unseen, as in
the prophecy, *the heavens declare the glory of God, and*

the firmament announces the works of His hands." [30]
The heaven of the beginning is not the heaven man sees,
but the spiritual meaning of that visible heaven.

In the light of such detailed interpretation of the crea-
tion *in principio* a reader like Bede would not have found
it difficult to see a hidden significance in the order of the
Hymn, which first states, "The eternal Lord established
the beginning of all wonders," then says:

> He first created for the sons of men
> heaven as a roof, the Holy Creator,
> then the middle-earth, the Ward of Mankind,
> the Eternal Lord, thereafter adorned
> for men on earth, Joy Almighty.

The second and the last divisions of the poem seem to
reflect the patristic distinction between the creation *in
principio* and the creation of heaven and earth for the
sons of men, which exists in time. In contrast to the adjec-
tive "eternal" of the second division, we have the adverbs,
"first," "then," and "thereafter" of the final division. Fur-
thermore, the one metaphorical description in the poem,
"heaven as a roof," might well have suggested to Bede the
spiritual symbolism that related the heaven seen by man
to the heaven of heavens. Ambrose says that if we wish
to discover the true nature of the heaven above us we
must ponder Isaiah 40:22: "God made heaven like to
a room." [31] In the same vein, Bede quotes St. Clement's
summary of the creation, "In the beginning when God
made the heaven and earth, he made it like to one house";
in the course of creation "the water, which was between
heaven and earth as a frozen solid, thawed"; the result-

ing firmament between the true heaven and the earth "God called heaven." Thus, what in the beginning "was one house, He divided into two regions; the reason for this division was that the upper region was the dwelling of angels; the lower, in truth, He granted to men." [32] Heaven and earth were given man as a home, and the heavens, which form the roof of that house, "declare the glory of God." They teach man to praise God and to live so that he may see the eternal heaven that was at the beginning. In short, God "first created for the sons of man/ heaven as a roof," as a reminder that "now we should praise the Ward of Heaven."

Finally, Caedmon says of the earth that the *eternal* God *adorned it* after He had made the heavens. Both the sequence of events and the image of God's adorning the earth are in accord with Scripture as the Fathers understood it. St. Ambrose says, for example, concerning the order of creation, "Primo fecit Deus, postea venustavit" (First God created, thereafter he adorned). [33] This order reveals that God is the only source of the beautiful. [34] Thus, the beauty of the earth comes from God and proclaims its Creator. [35] The earth in its beauty, like the heavens, reminds us to praise God and to think of the uncorrupted beauty of the eternal. The order of phrasing in the *Hymn,* "the middle-earth . . . thereafter He adorned," reflects Ambrose's understanding of the order of creation, the leading idea of which is that "we should praise the Ward of Heaven."

The end of the *Hymn* returns us to its beginning. There Caedmon rightly sings first of man's need to praise God, the Creator. The Creator is the Trinity, the Might of the Fatherhood, the Wisdom of the Word, the Perfection of the Holy Spirit. The mystery of the Trinity demands our wonder and our praise. Caedmon gives now another reason for praise: that though He was timeless, the eternal Lord in His Love chose to create a beginning, not only of eternal things, but also of temporal things. For He created the heavens to be as a roof for mankind in token of the spiritual heaven above, his home. The visible heavens not only declare the glory of God, but also teach man to praise Him. Man's dwelling place in time, the middle-earth, God afterward adorned so that man might perceive the Origin of beauty, God the Creator, and give thanks. The theme of the poem, explicitly stated at the beginning, is carried out implicitly in the underlying meanings suggested in the poem. Moreover, this thematic development is carried out in the details of word choice. As the three epithets that signify the Trinity are reflected in the tripartite division of the poem as a whole, so the poet's use of the remaining epithets for God seems further to reveal his adaptation of form to substance.

Caedmon first calls God the "Ward of Heaven," that is, of the *coelum coeli,* where He dwells eternally, Protector of His angels and saints. Next he speaks of Him as "the Eternal Lord," in the context of His establishing the beginning of all things; the epithet emphasizes the mystery of the creation of time by the Timeless. Only when Caedmon turns to the actual creation of heaven and earth for man does he call God the "Holy Creator"; it

is in the visible works of God that man, inexorably bound
in time and space, sees his Maker. With the mention of
the earth, in contrast to the first epithet, "Ward of
Heaven," Caedmon now calls God the "Ward of Man-
kind." The earth is man's temporal dwelling place; God
is the Protector Who will lead him from the earth to his
true home in heaven. To emphasize the greatness of the
Protector He is again called the *Eternal Lord*, heedful
of His people, but unknowable to a mind bound in time.
The final epithet, *Frea Almihtig* (Almighty Joy or Al-
mighty Lord), returns us to the thematic statement at
the beginning of the poem. For *frea* means both joy and
Lord, as God is both man's joy and his Lord. The true
pleasure of man is to rejoice in the Creator. To sing of
the creation, is, in fact, to rejoice in God, to praise Him
as "we now should do."

The possibility of deliberate word selection in the
Hymn links the English poem to Christian Latin poetry,
with its problem of adapting a pagan vocabulary to new
uses. And Bede's contrast between Caedmon's songs
and the lying songs of others suggests that Bede thought
of Caedmon as the first in England to call the poetic dic-
tion of his ancestors out of foreign bondage back into the
service of the Master. The *Hymn* itself reveals that Caed-
mon is not content to give a simple, literal translation of
biblical terms. A study of the diction of the poem serves
to suggest the deliberate employment for Christian pur-
poses of the pagan vocabulary of native heroic poetry.
The vocabulary of Caedmon's *Hymn* is, in fact, likely to
be the most striking aspect of the poem for the modern

reader, who feels a certain clash between the military, even pagan, connotations of the epithets for God and the Christian idea of God the Creator. Thus, God is called "Ward of Heaven, Ward of Mankind." God establishes the *ord* (point or beginning), a word of military connotations. Caedmon refers to the earth as the "middle-earth," a word perhaps related to the cosmogony of Germanic myth.

In discussing Caedmon's choice of his epithets for God no estimate may be made of how much or how little pagan connotation remains as effective counterpoint to the Christian idea expressed. Study of Caedmon's adaptation of a pagan poetic diction is handicapped by the lack of recorded pre-Christian pagan verse. We cannot be sure how much has been changed and modified in the process of Christian transmission.[36] As a result, no absolute standards of comparison exist as they do for Latin Christian poetry. Caedmon's choice of the epithet for God, "Ward of Heaven," may have derived either from a similar biblical term, translated from the Latin in a sermon Caedmon may have heard, or from ancestral poetry.[37] In his use of the term, with its connotations of a ruler protecting his followers from armed assault, he may simply have been thinking of the King of Heaven, the Duke of the Celestial Host, Who protected His throne and His followers from Lucifer. On the other hand, he may have been guided in his choice of words by memory of the heroic king of his native history and fable. It is not certain, but it seems probable, that his choice depended in large part upon the appropriateness of the pagan word to its new Christian context. If, as seems probable, the epithet "ward" retained connotations of the activities of the heroic king, it would have served admirably to represent an important symbolic meaning of God.

The connotative force of the first epithet is enforced by Caedmon's selection of the phrase *ord astealde* to describe the creation of the beginning. In its most concrete meaning *ord* refers to the point of the sword, but this military denotation serves an important figurative purpose. In patristic commentary the fact was stressed that the beginning is not yet in time, "for the beginning of a house is not yet the house." Similarly the point of the sword is not the sword. Moreover, *ord* also refers to the front of battle, the foremost point, which the heroic king first establishes and where he makes his stand to the end. The establishment of this *ord,* or point of battle, does not constitute the battle, but it does represent the beginning of the battle. Derived from this is the compound *ord-fruma,* which is used in OE poetry to refer both to God, the Creator, and to an earthly prince.[38]

The epithet *wuldorfæder* (Glory-Father) may fit, though perhaps more doubtfully, into the pattern of military or heroic connotation, contrasting with and enforcing the underlying Christian meaning. The Glory of God is a Christian commonplace; the heroic king also fought for glory (*wuldor*). The glory of God is nowhere more manifest to men than in His creation; the glory and fame of a king of heroic myth was nowhere more apparent than in his words and deeds when, before battle, he established the battlefront. But beyond the reputation gained in the forefront of battle the glory of the heroic king sprang from his reputation as a protector, a ward, of his people—at least that is the impression one gains from *Beowulf,* although the impression is not decisive, since the heroic motifs in *Beowulf* seem themselves to have been adapted to a Christian purpose. At any rate, Caedmon appears with some degree of artistry to have contrived by his choice of epithets a counterpoint of connotations suggesting the kingliness of God, Who is, in fact, the True King. The idea is, of course, Christian, whatever were the original connotations of the words.[39]

Caedmon's choice of the epithet "middle-earth" to signify the earth on which man dwells may reflect the pagan cosmogony of Germanic myth. Therein the earth was pictured as set between the home of the gods above and the home of their enemies, the giants, below. But Aldhelm in his Riddle 100, *Creatura,* speaks of penetrating the secrets of the Thunderer above, and of seeing below the earth Tartarus.[40] For the earth in the Christian spiritual cosmology stood midway between heaven and hell, considered as the ends of man's activity on earth. Man himself was created, according to Augustine, "in the middle of things, below God and above the bodily." [41] As Olympus, a word of pagan concept, could be used to suggest the Mount of Sion, the word "middle-earth," though it may originally have expressed a notion of pagan myth, was most useful in suggesting that the earth was created for man. On the middle-earth man journeys toward Jerusalem above or loses his way and ends in Babylon below.

Caedmon's inspired effort to adapt pagan poetic diction to the demands of Christian meaning is in accord with the practice of the Latin Christian poets, and particularly with that of his fellow English poet, Aldhelm. What he is doing accords also with Augustine's willingness, in theory, to make practical use of human means in the instruction of men. If a phrase of Caedmon's reflected, as was unavoidable, any phrase of pagan heroic poetry, so much the better, because the Christian meaning would gain in symbolic strength from use of the memorable pagan phrase—that is, if one loved the truth and not the word. The Christian had to accept the fact that his language had been spoken by men who did not know the teachings of the Church. He could, however, by exploiting the residual symbolic force of words, make a providential virtue of pagan necessity. If those who heard Caedmon's *Hymn* perceived in his epithets a reflection of ancestral poetry, their minds were actually being prepared, even though unconsciously, through the memory of the well-known and the poetically admired, to receive the Christian truth embodied in the pagan phrase. In restoring to the Master what is rightfully His, the poet takes from the Egyptians whatever is of worth; for example, the image of the true and good king of pagan poetry. Like Aldhelm's reported singing of the old songs to gain hearers for the Gospel,[42] Caedmon's employment of words rich in the connotations of heroic pagan poetry was justified by a very practical theory.

Everything being considered, there seem to be grounds for Bede's justification of Caedmon's *Hymn* as divinely inspired. The miracle lies not in the details of the angelic visitation, but in the concrete, empirical truth, as Bede saw it, that a man unlearned in Scripture, with its great intellectual demands, had the insight to proclaim what he never formally learned. Caedmon's dream, unsupported, might well have been dismissed; in accordance with Gregory the Great's principles dreams were in general looked upon with suspicion.[48] But the poem itself was visible evidence of unseen grace. Whatever guess may be made about Caedmon's own understanding of what he wrote and about the sources—sermons and the like—which might have supplied him with his material, the fact remains that the poem demonstrably contains the meaningful beauty that Bede associated with Scripture, the basic model of the beautiful. By employing the techniques established to reveal the truth and beauty of Scripture, it has been possible to show that to the pious mind determined to find hints of thematic truth, the form and diction of the *Hymn* would have given such hints.

On the other hand, the modern reader will wish to find a source—other than angelic—for Caedmon's inspiration. Caedmon was, of course, both illiterate and uninstructed when he composed the *Hymn*, but he was a Christian and he went to church. Simple as this fact may appear to be, it is a sufficient explanation of Caedmon's source of inspiration: his poem was the result of a long gestation of ideas and of unconscious imitation. In church, he would have had explained to him his creed and the meaning of the words, let us say, of the Preface; also he would have heard homilies, many of them translations of the Latin homilies of Augustine, Basil, Ambrose, Gregory. These homilies were, in general, exegetical in method; indeed many of the commentaries, cited above, exist as connected series of homilies. In addition it is likely that Caedmon possessed a powerful memory, more common than uncommon in the days before printing. St. Augustine takes for granted feats of memory staggering to the modern mind; in his *De catechizandis rudibus,* for example, he advises the instructor when he reviews biblical history for the catechumen not to recite the Bible from Genesis through Acts "verbatim as he has committed them to memory." [44] Facility of memory and the opportunity frequently to hear homilies, some presumably on the subject of the creation, would have been sufficient to afford a nonmiraculous genesis for the *Hymn.* The angelic vision would have served as a catalytic agent to precipitate ideas stored in Caedmon's memory, and he himself would have been unaware of the process until it flowered. His later poetry, written under direct monastic influence, was a result of imitation. As Bede explains, Abbess Hild had Caedmon "taught the whole course and succession of biblical history; he, then, remembering what he had learned in listening, and like to an innocent animal chewing the cud turned it all into delightful poetry."

Doctrine and Poetry

Another problem still remains: What is the likelihood that Caedmon's poetry would have been read "exegetically," for its underlying meaning? To answer this question it is necessary to reconstruct the attitude of mind which looked toward the skies and saw them proclaim the glory of God. This is difficult. The modern man may, with Keats, see in the heavens symbols of high romance; normally he does not see in them the precise and ordered symbols, which, organized through the interpretation of Scripture, appeared to the medieval man. Yet if the modern reader is to judge the works of the Christian poets of the Middle Ages he must make an effort at such historical reconstruction.

A grasp of the principles of Augustine's theory of literature helps at least to remove "surprise" that Caedmon's poetry is "subtle." Caedmon's poem is, in fact, not subtle; rather it is enigmatic and allusive. This style is the natural result of the influence upon Caedmon of a Christian ideal that pervaded the consciousness of Western Christendom. The "subtlety" results from the Augustinian resolution of two apparently opposite attitudes: that of late classical rhetoric, with its interest in elegancies and refinements, and that of Christian rhetoric, with its insistence on discovering single-mindedly, through whatever confusion, an underlying meaning consonant with the Faith. In Bede's view—and in Caedmon's view, because he was Christian—poetry that did not force the mind to an intense appreciation of such underlying truth was without function.

Furthermore, to recall the apparent complexity of

the English *Be Domes Dæg* is to suggest that Caedmon's unlearned audience may very reasonably be granted such awareness of symbolic meaning as would be necessary even partially to understand the verbal and stylistic potentialities of the *Hymn*. In his reading of the poem Bede would have been guided by Christian theory of literature, which would have led him automatically to look for the underlying meaning of angelically inspired verse. The letter of the *Hymn* for Bede could have meant only a shell to be cracked for the kernel of hidden meaning that alone would have given the poem the Christian beauty demanded by its angelic inspiration. The English poems already considered seem to have been written by poets governed by the same theory as that which governed Bede. Certainly they expected that their audiences would, in varying degrees, be able to grasp the meaning implicit in such a poem as Caedmon's *Hymn*.

Unfortunately these results cannot be checked by returning with any certainty to one of the long works of biblical inspiration ascribed to Caedmon by Bede. The manuscript that is sometimes editorially named after Caedmon is not so named by its original compiler. Nevertheless, the first poem therein, *Genesis*, has by many scholars been ascribed to Caedmon. If nothing else, we may safely call it a Caedmonian poem, for, as Bede points out, "Many another in the English nation followed Caedmon's lead in making songs, firmly fixed in Faith." Thus the *Genesis* poem should serve our purposes reasonably well. Its length and its direct relation to the Bible should serve to test the validity of the hypothesis that the Christian poet who wrote in English was intimately aware of the symbolic meaning of the Bible and expected his audience to share in this awareness. If the Caedmonian *Genesis* is, as it has often been called, a mere paraphrase of a portion of the biblical Genesis, it will not only be useless for checking the hypothesis but will even suggest that this hypothesis is too ambitious. The length of the ensuing chapter suggests that, at least in purpose, it is devoted to showing that the Caedmonian *Genesis* is very far from being a mere paraphrase.

NOTES TO CHAPTER IV

1. The translation follows the OE version of the *History,* ed. T. Miller (London, 1890–   ). For the *Hymn* see *Three Northumbrian Poems,* ed. A. H. Smith (London, 1933).
2. Isidore of Seville, "De Poetis," *Etymologiae,* Lindsay, *op. cit.,* VIII, vii. See Smith, *op. cit.,* p. 14. The primacy of biblical poetry is enunciated by Jerome. (See the Preface to Eusebius' *Chronicle, PL,* 27, 36; Preface to Job, *PL,* 28, 1081.) See Isidore's "De Metris," *Etymologiae,* I, xxxix, 11. Christian writings contain many examples of the achievement of knowledge through divine inspiration. See Augustine's preface to his *De doctrina;* his *De civitate Dei,* XVIII, xlii; and *De doctrina,* IV, vii, 15-21; also Cassian, *De institutis cenoborium,* V, xxxiii.
3. It is most instructive to read C. L. Wrenn, *The Poetry of Caedmon* (London, 1947), p. 9: "At first the Hymn may seem to have little intrinsic worth as poetry. Yet the more one reads it and allows it to become assimilated in one's mind, the more one feels it has qualities of balanced and rhythmic grandeur which still have some poetic appeal"; and then to read the review by George Kane in *MLR,* XLIII (1948), 250-252: "The Hymn has hardly enough literary merit to allow of discussing it at any length as a piece of poetry. . . . Finally, not everyone will be as certain of the high literary quality of Caedmon's poem as either Bede or Professor Wrenn appears to be."
4. Kane, *op. cit.,* p. 251. Kane is quite rightly protesting against Wrenn's conjecture that the miracle had primarily "artistic" interest (p. 12); but Kane's remark has itself pejorative implications against which it is well to put such a vigorous defense of the purposes of early Christian writers as that by Kuhnmuench, *op. cit.,* pp. 3-4. See De Labriolle, *op. cit., passim,* also Rand, *op. cit.,* Ch. VI.
5. He translates Caedmon's hymn into Latin prose. The remark is found only in the Latin original, of course (*Historia ecclesiastica,* ed. C. Plummer, I, 259-260): "Hic est sensus, non autem ordo ipse uerborum, quae dormiens ille canebat; neque enim possunt carmina, quamuis optime conposita, ex alia in aliam linguam ad uerbum sine detrimento sui decoris ac dignitatis transferri."

Doctrine and Poetry

6. See Spicq, *op. cit.*, pp. 10-30; Smalley, *op. cit.* (1st ed.), pp. xiv-xv; D. Robertson and B. Huppé, *"Piers Plowman" and Scriptural Tradition* (Princeton, 1951), pp. 1-20; De Labriolle, *op. cit.*, pp. 408-409; Kuhnmuench, *op. cit.*, p. 2.

7. The last part of Augustine's *Confessions* (XI-XIII) consists in commentary on the opening of Genesis, verses basic to his faith, thus part of his spiritual autobiography. Compare Aelfric's "On the Old and New Testament" and "Preface to Genesis," in his *The Heptateuch*, ed. Crawford, *op. cit.*, pp. 15-29 and 76-80. See also Augustine's *De catechizandis rudibus;* Eucherius, *Instructiones ad Salonium, PL,* 50, 773.

8. Spicq, *op. cit.*, pp. 30-31; M. Laistner, "Bede as a Classical and Patristic Scholar," in *Transactions of the Royal Historical Society,* 4th ser., XVI (1933), 79-94.

9. Bede, "Preface" to the *Hexameron, PL,* 91, 9-11.

10. Ambrose, *Hexameron, PL,* 14, 136.

11. Eustathius, *In hexameron S. Basilii latina metaphrasis, PL,* 53, 868-869. Cf. Augustine, *Confessions,* XI, iii, 5.

12. It was, of course, understood that the Latin was itself a translation, but a translation felt to possess something of the beauty of the original. The Greek Septuagint was felt to be divinely inspired, but although Augustine in the *De doctrina* gives the Septuagint precedence over the Latin, he used the Latin in his study of biblical eloquence. The weight of his authority was sufficient to sanction the letter of the Latin.

13. Eustathius, *PL,* 53, 870.

14. Ambrose, *PL,* 14, 137.

15. *Confessions,* XII, xiv, 17.

16. De Bruyne, *op. cit.*, I, 36, and *passim.*

17. Ambrose, *PL,* 14, 141.

18. *De rebus ecclisiasticis, PL,* 114, 948. The formula of the Preface, "Vere dignum," is found in the earliest liturgies. See, for example, the Gregorian liturgy (*PL,* 78, 24-25); see also the *Catholic Encyclopedia, s.v.,* "Preface." The office of the Mass seems a more likely influence on the yet secular Caedmon than the monastic office of the hours suggested by I. Gollancz, *The Caedmon Manuscript* (Oxford, 1927), p. lxi. The *nu* is probably a generalized, not a specific, expression.

19. *PL,* 50, 1287.

20. "On the Old and New Testament" and "Preface to Genesis" in

Crawford, *op. cit.*, pp. 16-17 and 78; "Sermon on the Creation," in the *Homilies of the Anglo-Saxon Church*, ed. B. Thorpe (London, 1849), I, 10.

21. Ambrose, *PL*, 14, 150: "*Et spiritus Dei superferebatur super aquas* . . . nos tamen cum sanctorum et fidelium sententia congruentes, Spiritum sanctum accipimus, ut in constitutione mundi operatio Trinitatis eluceat. Praemisso enim quia *in principio fecit Deus coelum et terram,* id est, in Christo fecit Deus, vel Filius Dei Deus fecit, vel per Filium Deus fecit; quia omnia per ipsum facta sunt, et sine ipso factum est nihil, supererat plenitudo operationis in Spiritu." Augustine, *De Genesi ad litteram,* I, vi, 12: "Et quemadmodum in ipso exordio inchoatae creaturae, quae coeli et terrae nomine, propter id quod de illa perficiendum erat, commemorata est, Trinitas insinuatur Creatoris, nam dicente Scriptura, *In principio fecit Deus coelum et terram;* intelligimus Patrem in Dei nomine, et Filium in principii nomine, qui non Patri, sed per seipsum creatae primitus ac potissimum spirituali creaturae, et consequenter etiam universae creaturae principium est: dicente autem Scriptura, *Et spiritus Dei ferebatur super aquam,* completam commemorationen Trinitatis agnoscimus.

22. Honorius of Autun, *Hexameron, PL,* 172, 254. For the Holy Spirit as the perfection of the work, see the phrase of Ambrose, n. 21, "plenitudo operationis in Spiritu." Bede translates Caedmon's three epithets as *potentiam, consilium, facta.* (See n. 5.)

23. Eustathius, *PL,* 53, 874.

24. Ambrose, *PL,* 14, 139: "Dedit ergo forman futuris annorum curriculis mundi primus exortus, ut ea lege annorum curriculis mundi primus exortus." Eustathius, *PL,* 53, 875.

25. *Confessions,* XII, viii, 8: "Sed illud coelum coeli tibi, Domine; terra autem quam dedisti filius hominum cernendam atque tangendam, non erat talis qualem nunc cernimus et tangimus."

26. Bede, *PL,* 91, 13-14.

27. Augustine, *Confessions,* XII, xi, 12.

28. *Ibid.,* XI, ix, 9.

29. Bede, *op. cit.,* 13-14.

30. Ambrose, *PL,* 14, 141.

31. *Ibid.,* 143-144. See Eustathius, *op. cit., PL,* 53, 876.

32. Bede, *PL,* 91, 19-20.

33. Ambrose, *PL,* 14, 148.

34. *Ibid., PL,* 14, 149 and 153.

35. Cassiodorus, *De anima*, XII, *PL*, 69, 1304.

36. See F. M. Stenton, *Anglo-Saxon England* (Oxford, 1947), p. 192: "The English poetry of the heathen age was first written down by Christian clerks, and most of it survives in texts which are affected by Christian ideas and imagery."

37. Scotus Erigena discusses in his *Expositiones, PL*, 122, 145-146, the meaning of the military figures used to represent heavenly beings.

38. For the various meanings of *ord* see C. Grein, *Sprachschatz*. The word *hlaford* may also have been in Caedmon's mind.

39. See Augustine's mirror of the true king in *De civitate Dei*, V, xxiv.

40. Ehwald, *op. cit.*, p. 146.

41. See above, Ch. III, n. 51.

42. See Ch. III, n. 11.

43. *Moralia, PL*, 75, 827: "Somnis non facile credendum. Cur daemon sanctorum corda somniis officere sinatur."

44. See also the *De doctrina*, 4, 7(5) and 2, 14(9); H. Chaytor, *From Script to Print* (Cambridge, 1945), pp. 115-119. See F. Magoun, "Bede's Story of Caedmon," *Speculum*, XXX (1955), 49-63.

Chapter V

THE CAEDMONIAN *GENESIS*

THE Caedmonian *Genesis* is found in a manuscript called variously the Junius MS, after its first editor, Junius, or the Caedmon MS, because it was supposed to contain a selection of the poems attributed to Caedmon by Bede. Although the manuscript itself nowhere alludes to Caedmon, the general anonymity of medieval manuscripts precludes any argument against Caedmonian authorship on this basis alone. But of the four poems in the manuscript the last, called *Christ and Satan,* must be excepted from Caedmonian authorship both on stylistic and on linguistic grounds. Stylistically, the second and third poems, called *Exodus* and *Daniel,* are sufficiently different from each other and from the first poem, called *Genesis,* to suggest not single, but multiple authorship. Finally, a portion of the *Genesis* itself (ll. 255-851), called *Genesis* B, has been proved to be an interpolation based on a late Saxon original. *Genesis* A (ll. 1-234 and 852-2936) alone remains as possibly Caedmonian.[1] But whether or not *Genesis* A is by Caedmon is unimportant for the purpose of checking the hypothesis that the Augustinian theory of literature aids in the study of OE Christian poetry. The problem in criticism is to show that *Genesis* A is Caedmonian in the sense that its purpose and method are the same as those which indirectly inspired Caedmon's *Hymn.*

A critical understanding of the poem is made difficult by the fact so little is certain about *Genesis* A except where the interpolated portion, *Genesis* B, begins and ends. This certainty marks the end of any real scholarly agreement. The identity of authorship of the first and second portions of *Genesis* A has been questioned; that is to say, *Genesis* A may consist of three or more fragments patched together scribally. Moreover, since *Genesis* A ends with the Sacrifice of Isaac and thus does not cover the whole of the biblical book, it has been supposed that the poem is not complete in the manuscript. In short, it would appear almost impossible to read *Genesis* A as a poem, so that the attempt at historical literary judgment seems almost desperate. Yet these problems may perhaps be resolved.

Since *Genesis* is a long poem, it will be helpful, for the sake of perspective, to outline it briefly. It begins with the exhortation to praise God, then describes how the angels lived with God in joy until Lucifer was cast into hell, while the faithful angels remained in concord. It tells of the empty places in heaven, and of how God determines to fill them with a new creation from what was still dark and empty. In these first 111 lines the poem has advanced only through the first verse of Genesis, as that verse was understood in the hexameral commentaries to include the creation of the angels.[2] In lines 111-234, the poem settles to a closer paraphrase of the biblical verses dealing with the works of the days (Gen. 1:2–2:14). After line 234 there is a lacuna in the manuscript, and the account of the creation is interrupted. *Genesis* B begins in the middle of a sentence, apparently spoken by God to Adam and Eve, forbidding them to eat of the fruit of the tree. The six hundred lines of this notable interpolation are an account of the assemblage of tortured devils in hell and their plan for revenge, which culminates in the Fall of Man, and a description of the Fall. After the account of the Fall, *Genesis* A resumes, without a break, paraphrasing Genesis 3:8–22:18; that is, the paraphrase extends from the episode of God's walking in Paradise to that of the Sacrifice of Isaac. Putting aside the problem of the purpose of the long interpolation, *Genesis* B, our study of *Genesis* A resolves itself into a consideration of the two parts, which are separated by the interpolation, to discover whether the intention of the first part is carried out in the second.[3] If we can discover what is intended in these parts of the poem, it may be possible to determine the reason for the interpolation. The general question may be stated thus: In the light of Augustinian theory of literature may the poem *Genesis* be shown to have a unifying theme which unites all parts of the poem and to which the interpolated portion is also appropriate?

Whatever the first hundred or more lines of *Genesis*

may be, they are not a "mere paraphrase" of Genesis. For this reason, and ignoring the fact that hexameral commentary included the creation of the angels as part of the implied meaning of the first verse of Genesis, some critics have assumed that the actual "paraphrase" begins only with the second hundred lines of the poem, the first hundred lines representing an introductory literary flourish with heavy overtones of "Teutonic flavor." Actually the beginning of the poem develops one aspect of the underlying meaning of the first verse of *Genesis*—a development that is perhaps to be explained by the absolute importance of that verse to Christian faith.

The first lines of the poem, furthermore, propose the same theme as in Caedmon's *Hymn,* man's duty to sing the praises of his Creator, the sum of man's primary duty:

> Us is riht micel   ðæt we rodera weard
> wereda wuldorcining   wordum herigen
> modum lufien.   He is magna sped
> heafod ealra   heahgesceafta
> frea ælmihtig.

For us it is greatly fitting that the Ward of the Heavens,/ the Glory-King of Hosts we praise with words,/ love with our hearts. He is great in might,/ the source of all the high creation,/ Joy Almighty./

Even more clearly than in the *Hymn* the lines reflect the Latin words of the Preface in the Mass: "Vere dignum et justum est, aequum et salutare, nos tibi semper et undique gratias agere, domine sancte, Pater omnipotens, aeterne Deus." It is the theme that we might expect from a poem on Genesis. For Genesis, as interpreted by the commenta-

tors, not only describes man's fall, but forecasts his re-
demption as well; and the promotion of man's duty to
praise God is the aim and logical conclusion of the tradi-
tional justification of God's ways in the story of the
Creation, Fall, and Redemption. The *Genesis* attributed
to Hilary of Arles, it may be recalled, begins in a similar
fashion; [4] and it may be relevant that Hilary's *Genesis,*
as it has survived, is also like the Caedmonian poem in
being limited to a part of Genesis. It traces the story
only to the Flood, as the English poem traces the story
to the Sacrifice of Isaac.

But the Flood may represent baptism, and the Sacrifice
of Isaac may represent the Redemption; each incident
in its symbolic meaning may have been intended as a
conclusion to a poem celebrating one of the underlying
meanings of Genesis. That is, both poems may be com-
plete and thematically intended. They would have as
their purpose, through figurative interpretation of a por-
tion of Genesis, to set forth man's duty to praise God.
Indeed, the hastiest reading of Hilary's *Genesis* should
be sufficient to dispel the misconception that it is an in-
complete paraphrase of Genesis. It begins, as noted, with
the thematic statement that man should give thanks to
God. The first thirty-nine lines are occupied with the
theme of the praise of God, the Creator, for his creation.
Lines 40-124 take up the subject of the works of the days,
through the creation of man, in a very free treatment of
the biblical verses. At line 125 Hilary begins an apos-
trophe to man, "the happy animal":

Doctrine and Poetry

O happy animal: of whom the right hand of the
   highest Thunderer
is Father; o happy, indeed, who takes from Olympus
both kind and form, if the evil vices of the world
deceive you not, nor beguiling error mislead you!
A divine spirit you will be, one led back to the
   heavenly and wondrous kingdom:
which promises the Father made to the just
   through His faithful mouth.

In lines 131-159, Hilary shows the glorious estate of man
in his superiority over other earthly creatures and in his
God-given gift of the world. From line 160 to line 184
he shows that man is responsible for sin and its accom-
panying evils, which were finally wiped out by God in
the Flood (185-190). From the Flood a better people
arose, like the children who sing in the fiery furnace, like
Daniel in the lion's den, like the kings and prophets (191-
200). He concludes with a figurative reference to baptism
(201-204):

> quamuis cuncta deo seruirent crimine victo,
> attamen antiqui etiamnum gutta veneni
> spargebat populos et erant vestigia fraudis,
> quae bonus abluerat doctor melioribus undis.

However much all served God, sin having been conquered,/
yet a spot of the ancient venom/ stained the people, and traces
of false remained/ which the Good Doctor had washed away
with the better waters.

When it is recalled that the Flood was understood to pre-
figure baptism; the ark, the Church of Christ; and Noah,
Christ Himself, Hilary's intention becomes clear.[5] A basic
reason for praising God rests in the spiritual history of

136

man. He was made to glorify God and to become worthy
to fill the places in heaven left vacant by the fallen angels.
When he understands the creation as it is set forth in
Genesis, man will understand his need to give thanks.
When he reflects further on the great spiritual truths
suggested in the Genesis, he will understand his pur-
pose in life even better. Man in disobedience fell from
his high estate, but God through His Son promised Re-
demption. These great spiritual events are found, one
historically and the other prophetically, in Genesis.
Daniel and the children in the fiery furnace, with whom
Hilary concludes, represent those who will be saved
through the blood of Christ as the Christian will be
saved by baptism.[6] The theme of Hilary's *Genesis* is that
it is right and good for man to praise his Creator because
of the high destiny that the Creator has prepared for him
and reserved for him through the Redemption in spite
of man's having turned from God. To understand Hilary's
poem it is necessary to think not so much of the literal
level of Genesis as of the Preface in the Mass, where the
fixed words, which are repeated at the beginning of the
poem, are to be followed by a variable development of
the multifarious reasons why it is right and good that man
worship God. Hilary's poem serves, briefly, the same
purpose. It shows what in Genesis the Christian may
find to convince him of God's mercy and bounty.

In similar fashion, the first hundred lines of the Caed-
monian *Genesis* take on shape and meaning when they
are related to a thematic purpose of revealing God's ways
to man so that he may truly understand the words of the

Preface. To demonstrate this thematic point it is necessary to consider the first hundred lines in detail.

The poem begins (1-14) with a thematic statement, *"Us is riht micel,"* directed toward man and pictures the blessedness of the inhabitants of heaven, the angels, who fulfill their being in praising God. The blessedness of the angels is summarized in line 14, "Wæs heora blæd micel." The repetition of the word *micel* in the two thematic statements serves to frame the passage rhetorically and to remind the reader of the Christian truth that in praising God man may share the glory possessed by angels. The poem continues (15-21) with a picture of the blessedness of the angels, but lines 22-23 introduce a sharply contrasting idea that the condition of blessedness continued only, "until some of the angels fell into heresy through pride." [7] The subject of the fall of the angels is now pursued, and hell, their eternal, joyless home, is described (24-26). In lines 12-46 a contrasting pattern of thought is established: the injunction that man praise God is enforced in the contrast between the blessedness of those who praised and the damnation of those who refused to glorify His name. This pattern of thought is stressed by another rhetorical balance of structure. Of the blessed angels it is said (12-14):

> Hæfdon gleam and dream
> and heora ordfruman   engla þreatas
> beorhte blisse. Wæs heora blæd micel!

They had brightness and joy/ and their Creator, the troops of angels,/ shining bliss. Was their glory great!

138

Of the evil angels when they are introduced (25) the poet says ironically and in rhetorical repetition, "Hæfdon gielp micel" (They had great boastfulness). The description of the plight of the angels ends (45-46) with a structural repetition of the same sentence pattern:

> Hæfdon hie [the fallen angels] wrohtgeteme
> grimme wið god gesomnod.   Him þæs grim lean becom!

They had much wrong,/ grim together against God. To them for this came a grim reward!

This rhetorical pattern serves to give prominence to the thematic contrast between the destiny of those who praise God and have joy and that of those who refuse to serve in praise and possess only a foolish boast, which leads to destruction. In the story of the angels man may find convincing proof that for him it is very right to praise the Ruler of Heaven.

Apparently the poet now proceeds to tell the story that has been summarized in the opening two passages, for lines 47-64 begin with the angels plotting rebellion and end with the anger of God against them. The next passage (65-77) tells of God's driving the fallen angels into hell and of their suffering. The contrasting joy in heaven of the angels who remained faithful to God and the harmony that remained in heaven after the evil ones were expelled are pictured in lines 78-86.[8] Finally, the result of the expulsion, the empty thrones of heaven, is described (86-91):

> Him on laste setl
> wuldorspedum welig   wide stodon
> gifum growende   on godes rice

beorht and geblædfæst   buendra leas
siððan wræcstowe   werige gastas
under hearmlocan   heane geforan.

Among them at last the thrones/ rich in glorious beauty widely
stood/ increasing in riches in the kingdom of God/ bright and
firm in glory deprived of dwellers/ after the wretched spirits
to the place of torment/ under evil bonds had thence pro-
ceeded.

The image of the empty thrones of heaven suggests that
the poet's purpose in retelling the story outlined in the
opening lines of the poem is to give prominence to the
theme of contrastive wrath and mercy. The fall of the
angels serves as a dreadful warning to man, but the
thrones they left empty give promise to man of citizen-
ship in heaven, if, through obedience, he proves himself
worthy.

The next lines (93-111) appear to conclude the intro-
ductory portion of the poem, since at line 112 the poet
begins his free paraphrase of the works of the days in
Genesis. The concluding lines of introduction explain
figuratively God's purpose in the creation as related to
the empty thrones in heaven and reiterate the theme of
God's mercy to man (93-103):

Then our Lord considered
in his wisdom how the illustrious creation,
the native regions, He might after settle
with a better band, the heavenly home,
which the boast-guilty had abandoned,
high in heaven. Therefore Holy God
under the sway of the heavens with his great might
desired that for them earth and sky
and the broad water would be established,

the world creation in recompense for the evil ones,
those traitors he had sent from His protection.[9]

The poet, in the manner of Caedmon's *Hymn,* distinguishes the creation "in the beginning," when only the spiritual heaven and its inhabitants were created, from the creation of man's visible world. For, by reversing the order of the first verse of Genesis—"heaven and earth"—he carefully indicates that he is referring in this passage to the visible creation: "Holy God," he says here, "desired that for them the earth, the heaven and broad waters were established," thus specifically indicating the creation of the world of earth, sky, and water. The poet further stresses this aspect of creation in the ensuing lines (104-111), which describe the empty idleness of the earth before it was illumined by the word of God. His figurative conception of God's purpose in creating the earth for man as distinct from His creation of the spiritual heaven is traditional. For example, Aelfric in his *On the Old and New Testament* explains that when Lucifer conspired against God:

> Then had he no seat to sit on: for no part of heaven would beare him: nor might there any kingdom be his against the will of God, who made all. Then perceived this proud one what his power was: sith he had no place to rest on; but fell downe, into deuill turned with all his complices, from the court of God to the paines of hell, as they deserued. Within six daies after this was done, Almighty God created man; *Adam* of the earth, with his owne hands, and gaue him soule; and *Eue* of *Adams* rib soone after: that they and their offspring with them might enjoy that faire estate which the deuill forfeited, if they duly obeyed their Maker.[10]

In His creation of the visible world for man God manifested his beneficence to men who through obedience and praise of God may enter into His kingdom. By stressing this aspect of God's creation the poet relates the story of the angels, both good and evil, to the liturgical truth that he expresses in the opening lines of the poem:

> Us is riht micel   ðæt we rodera weard
> wereda wuldorcining   wordum herigen
> wordum lufien!

The introductory lines of *Genesis*, it is clear, are not a paraphrase of Genesis, but a free, thematic expansion of the truth derived from the first verse of Genesis that the angelic creation is related to human creation in revealing to man his proper duty of praising God. This thematic statement provides something of a guide to the remainder of the poem, which, to be one poem in the Caedmonian tradition, should be unified by a single thematic concept.

With line 112, after the introductory generalization just discussed, the poet begins his free paraphrase of the biblical account of the works of the days (Gen. 1:1–2:14). He stays fairly close to the biblical text, but by treating details with a vigorous freedom, he not only achieves vivid contemporary translation in the English vernacular, but also manages to give some sense of the underlying significance of the verses. The manner of this paraphrase may be indicated most simply by examining lines 116-125. These lines have been held up to ridicule by Legouis, a ridicule which has been approvingly repeated by De Bruyne: "One cannot find," says Legouis, "a more handsome lesson of the difference between grandiose verbiage and the true sublime" than in the passage in question.[11] A paraphrase of Gen. 1:2-3, the guilty lines come almost at the beginning of the body of the *Genesis* poem (116-125).

> Folde wæs þa gyt
> græs ungrene. Garsecg þeahte
> sweart synnihte side and wide
> wonne wægas. þa wæs wuldortorht
> heofonweardes gast ofer holm boren
> miclum spedum. Metod engla heht
> lifes brytta leoht forð cuman
> ofer rumne grund. Raþe wæs gefylled
> heahcyninges hæs, him wæs halig leoht
> ofer westenne, swa se wyrhta bebead.

The earth was yet/ grass ungreen. The ocean covered/ in black eternal night wide and far/ the dark waves. Then was the Glory-Torch,/ the spirit of the Heaven-Ward over the waters borne/ with great speed. The Lord of Angels commanded,/ the Apportioner of Life, the light to come forth/ over the broad ground. Quickly was accomplished/ the command of the High King. For Him was the holy light/ over the waste [*or* west], as the Creator bade.

The poet here compactly translates into the OE poetic idiom both the letter and the significance of the biblical verses. For, as Legouis and De Bruyne have not observed, the poet suggests one, of the underlying meanings of the second verse of Genesis that was understood to explain the first verse by differentiating the heaven "in the beginning" from all that which remained inchoate and from which the visible, temporal world was created. Any historically accurate judgment will grant that the poet's phrase, "The earth was yet grass ungreen," is an effective and meaningful equivalent for "The earth was idle and empty," particularly in the light of the exegetical connotations of the biblical phrase.

Moreover, the poet's translation derives further effectiveness from the symbolic values of "grass" and of "green." When Augustine wishes to explain that the earth was nothing "in the beginning," yet at the same time was awaiting the act of creation which would give it being, he employs a striking figure: "The earth," he says, "was not apt for cultivation" (*non erat apta ad culturum*).[12] Through this figure he expresses graphically the underlying truth that the earth was empty and without form because it had not yet been filled with the vivifying Spirit of God, so that it could not be planted and made fruitful with the seed of God's word. The poet expresses the same truth in the figure of the earth as ungreen grass; that is, the earth without the vivifying force of the Spirit of God is like grass without its living mark of identity, its greenness. The greenness of the earth symbolizes the earth given being through the vivifying Spirit; its lack of greenness symbolizes its spiritual formlessness, not a loss of color but the as yet unrealized potentiality of receiving color. The poet's figure emphasizes the absolute position of God in relation to all created things and thus suggests man's need to praise Him.

The symbolic resources of the passage have a further dimension in the poet's likening of the darkness that covers the waters to the blackness of eternal night. For in this figure the poet suggests that the darkness, described in Genesis 1:2, is to be contrasted with the informing light of God, as nonbeing is contrasted with being. The darkness covering the void is the positive darkness of nonbeing. It is a positive darkness because it is the opposite of the light of being and, with wordplay on *synn* (sin), may be likened to the black night of sin, also defined as that which is without good. This darkness covers, says the poet, "the wan waves." The adjective "wan" implies absence of color, so that the "wan waves" are parallel in symbolic meaning with the "ungreen grass." The darkness of nonbeing, the poet suggests in his figure, covers the colorless uncreate, the wan void, which is to take form and become the visible world.[13] The wan waves of the uncreate signify chaos but not dark-night.

The figure of the eternal night of nonbeing is further amplified in the poet's description of the Holy Spirit borne over the waters. The Holy Spirit is called the *wuldortorht*, the Glory-Torch, that is, the sun dispelling the darkness of night and revealing the form of the creation, at God's command bringing light to the darkness.[14] Finally, to describe the light of being informing the darkness, the poet says that the light came forth *ofer westenne*. The noun *westenne* offered the poet the possibility of wordplay, since it means waste but in its first syllable suggests the west. The light of the sun to which the Spirit was likened shines over the waste—the purposeless, the uninformed, which will be made, through the informing power of the light, into a garden, rich in the greenness of

True Being. A similar underlying meaning is suggested if we consider the significance of the light of the sun shining in the west as opposed to the east. According to Eucherius of Lyons, the east represents the Saviour, "because from that part the light springs." The west represents "a lack of the better life." [15] The Holy Spirit transforms the waste through his vivifying force as the eastern sun fills the cold west with the warmth of charity. The poetic figures that suggest the mystery of the second verse of Genesis all have an additional moral implication for man in his relation to his Creator.

The epithets applied to God in the passage under discussion recall the figurative picture of God, the Defender of Heaven, drawn in the introduction: here He is called the Ruler of angels, the Ward of heaven, the High King. Apart from their effect in unifying the poem itself, the military and kingly epithets serve also to emphasize the underlying connection of the first and second verses of Genesis. The light, the Holy Spirit, Who is born over the waters, is a person of the Trinity, God, the king of the eternal heaven that existed before the creation of the temporal universe. The echoing of the epithets for God thus suggests the identity of the Trinity, the mystery testified to by the beginning of Genesis. The double function of the epithets, structural and symbolic, is best illustrated in the poet's use of the epithet *lifes brytta,* which suggests God's figurative kingly function as the treasure-divider, the breaker of treasure, apportioning eternal happiness, *life,* to his faithful angelic hosts; but the epithet also suggests God's function as creator, divider of life; the act of creation is a dividing of light from dark, being from nonbeing.

Detailed study of lines 116-125, therefore, suggests that a poet capable of such careful employment of figure and epithet cannot be dismissed offhandedly as a writer of verbiose paraphrase. In purpose, at least, he is seeking to inspire in his audience understanding of the significance of the Bible.

The paraphrase of Genesis continues through verse 2:14, but after line 234 of *Genesis* there is a lacuna in the manuscript, and *Genesis* B begins in the middle of a sentence apparently spoken by God to Adam and Eve. *Genesis* B tells of the Fall. *Genesis* A (852-2936), resumes with a free paraphrase of Genesis, verses 3:8, God's walking in the garden, to 22:18, the Sacrifice of Isaac.

The method of these last two thousand lines of *Genesis* A is on the whole closer to that of the paraphrase of the works of the days (112-234) than to that of the introductory lines. But what the poet intends in his paraphrase cannot be illustrated by a random sampling, for apart from the obvious changes made necessary by his manner of translation he develops certain passages with an amplitude that suggests the development of the opening lines of the poem rather than free paraphrase. Thus the fact that lines 852-2936 follow the biblical story fairly closely should not make us overlook the modifications and changes which the poet effects in the story. Some of these modifications may be readily explained as designed to make the biblical story clearer or more dramatic. There are also small modifications or alterations which have as their purpose the inclusion of exegetical material. As an example of such alteration we may cite the poet's allusion to the city built by Cain as the *first* earthly city, a fact which is not to be found in the biblical verses but is to be found in the commentaries. Another such exegetical but not biblical fact is represented in the poet's explanation that the man slain by Lamech (Gen. 4:23), unnamed in the Bible, was actually Cain.[16] Such alterations, whether dramatic or exegetical in purpose, are readily explained as part of vital and significant paraphrase.

On the other hand, the poem contains certain alterations, additions, condensations, and omissions which seem to go beyond the widest conception of meaningful paraphrase. Many passages cannot be explained even by assuming vaguely that the poet was attempting a non-Augustinian literary embellishment. Why, for example, should he choose to give one complete set of genealogies (Gen. 4:17–5:31) and of another genealogy (Gen. 10:1–11:26) choose to give only excerpts? Again, what principle governs the selection of passages for elaboration, an elaboration, as we shall see, which goes far beyond paraphrase and becomes, rather, amplification in the manner of the introductory story of the angels? What principle governs the omission of many portions of chapters included in the scope of the poem? Finally, did the poet intend a complete paraphrase of Genesis, or did he intend to end his poem with the Sacrifice of Isaac? These problems make necessary a detailed study of the amplifications, modifications, condensations, and omissions in the poem to discover whether collectively they reveal an underlying thematic purpose that will explain not only their own reason for being but also the poet's intention in writing the *Genesis.*

Genesis A, as has been mentioned, resumes directly from the interpolated *Genesis* B, with the biblical account of the shame of Adam and Eve when God walked in the garden and the account of God's subsequent expulsion of Adam and Eve from the garden. The first significant addition to the biblical narrative in the continuation of *Genesis* A occurs after the poetic version of God's sentence of exile. The lines in question (939-940) constitute a brief expository statement without parallel in the biblical text. The lines seem, in effect, to mark a transition or introduction to a new section of narrative:

> Hwæt! we nu gehyrað hwær us hearmstafas
> wraðe onwocon and woruldyrmðo.

> Yea! we hear now in what manner the rods of evil upon us/
> beat in wrath and the worldly afflictions.

The phrase *"Hwæt! we nu gehyrað"* is a conventional type of introductory epic formula in OE poetry. The poet seems to employ this device first to mark a stage in the development of the poem and second to indicate that the theme of the ensuing narrative will be the growth of evil in the world.

The division in the poem between the events before and those after the expulsion reflects a division made, for example, in Bede's *Hexameron,* where Book I ends with

149

the expulsion of Adam and Eve from Paradise and Book II commences with the beginnings of man's life in the world. The biblical story is now concerned, in its underlying significance, with the drama of man's life on earth as he finds his way back to Paradise or loses his way forever in the earthly kingdom. For this reason Bede introduces Book II of his *Hexameron* with a contrast between the joys of Paradise and the afflictions of the world: "Here now after the delights of Paradise and the guilt of the first lying deceit, are related the needs of this world and this mortal life." [17] The exegetical division serves to give thematic consequence to the biblical story of Cain and Abel and of the progeny of Adam and Eve in general. This thematic division seems to be reflected in the external form of the poem.

That the poet's intention was deliberately to suggest the exegetical theme is given further plausibility by his treatment (941-964) of God's clothing of Adam and Eve, His expelling them from the garden and setting a guardian over the gate of Paradise (Gen. 3:21-24). He is content with a fairly literal paraphrase (941-948) of the clothing and expulsion, but in describing the guarding of the gates by the angel with the flaming sword he makes a considerable addition to the biblical text. The addition takes the form of a comment on the meaning of the expulsion from Eden (948-964):

> No wicked one may enter there,
> guilt-stained man, but the guardian has
> might and power, he who that illustrious life,
> dear to men, holds for God.

Yet the Almighty wished not all
comforts to withdraw from Adam and Eve,
Father at the beginning, though He may have turned
    from them,
but He as a comfort to them permitted still to remain
the sky-roof adorned with the holy stars,
and to them He gave land treasures broad.
He commanded for the ever-wedded pair the sea
    and earth,
for each of the coming generations of their progeny,
in their worldly need, to feed them their fruits.
They lived then after sin in a more sorrowful land,
a dwelling place and home less rich
in every comfort than was their first habitation
from which after the deed they had been driven.

The poet's commentary serves to generalize, to give allegorical significance to, the keeping of the gate by God's appointed angel; this becomes in the poem symbolic of the exile into the world of all mankind, of the affliction from which mankind may recover only by living in accord with God's law and through the sacrifice of Christ. The reasons for the poet's expository addition are explicable in reference to patristic commentary on the relevant biblical passages.

Bede in his commentary on the Pentateuch deals succinctly with the expulsion of Adam and Eve from Eden. He explains that God, in clothing Adam and Eve, symbolically clothed them with "the mortality of the body." In the cherubim whom He placed at the gate, God signified "fullness of knowledge." The turning sword, which the cherubim held "for guarding the way to the tree of life, signifies bodily afflictions." In the guarding of the gate God set forth symbolically the truth that "no one may come to the tree of life, except through these two things, suffering of afflictions and fullness of knowledge, that is, through the love of God and neighbor: for the fullness of the law is Charity." In his *Hexameron,* commenting on the same verses, Bede, following Augustine, gives an alternative explanation. He considers the guarding of the gate to symbolize the comforting promise of "blessed life." Without the promise of such life, "the sinner would have to dwell everywhere in misery," but cherubim and sword signify that "return is permitted to the heavenly home from which we departed through the folly of the lie and of desire for carnal pleasure." [18]

The lines in the poem seem to reflect the commentary in the poetic statement that, though no sinner may pass through the gates, God does not utterly desert man: He does not take away, for example, the "holy stars," which, as in Caedmon's *Hymn,* are symbols of the heavenly home to which man may return. The expulsion from Eden represents the beginning of earthly affliction for man (961-964), but, if it is endured in patience and charity and with the aid of divine grace, this very affliction may be the means by which he can find his way home to God (954-956). The evil man, through his own guilty loss of citizenship in the native land, may never return through the gates (948-950), but man is not abandoned by God, Who gives him, as the poet shows, what is needful to sustain life. It remains for man to use these goods to the end that God's will may be served. In this transitional passage connecting the narrative of the Fall with the narrative of man's life on earth, the poet implies the theme of Christian use of earthly goods.

The poet immediately employs this theme in the story of Cain and Abel, which he introduces next in a brief passage (969-971) without counterpart in the biblical text:

> Us cyðað bec
> hu þa dædfruman   dugeþa stryndon
> welan and wiste   willgebroðor.

The lines are obscure and require interpretation. The first half-line, "Books tell us," presents no difficulties. If the line is indefinite in intention, it must serve, like the "Yea, we have heard" (939) of the preceding passage, as a formal device to emphasize the division already indicated. If any specific books are meant, they must be books that have to do with Genesis—commentaries, hexameral expositions, homilies, or the like. The line would then indicate the poet's concern with the patristic interpretation of Scriptures. In this event the phrase "Books tell us" serves to remind the reader that the story to be unfolded has a significance more important than the story itself.

The remainder of the passage, however, is obscure, because the subject, *dædfruman,* and the verb, *stryndon,* have each two very different connotations in OE poetry. *Stryndon* may refer both to the producing of goods and to the begetting of children. *Dædfruman,* literally "deed-creators," is found only five times in extant OE verse (always in the singular). In *Beowulf,* 2090, it is used to signify an evildoer; whereas in *Andreas,* 75 and 1455, it

153

is used as an epithet for God, and in the late *Five
Boroughs* poem, as an epithet for King Edmund of Eng-
land. The only other recorded use in OE poetry is in
our passage, where it is found in the plural.[19] Uncertainty
is increased in examining the context of the passage.
If *dædfruman* refers to the subject of the preceding
verses, Adam and Eve, the first evildoers, the passage
says that they begot (*stryndon*) the brothers, Cain and
Abel. On the other hand, if *dædfruman* refers to the
subject of the ensuing narrative, the brothers Cain and
Abel, the passage says that these were the first doers
who produced goods for earthly use.

The reader having the subject of Adam and Eve in
mind is naturally inclined to translate:

> Books tell us
> how the first evildoers of men begot
> wealth and nourishment, the brothers of the will.

This interpretation of *dædfruman* as referring to Adam
and Eve would involve no difficulty if the only object of
the verb, *stryndon*, were *willgebroðor*, that is, Cain and
Abel, their sons. But since the object of *stryndon* must
also be, in this reading, "wealth" and "nourishment," a
reconsideration of the passage, with *dædfruman* refer-
ring to Cain and Abel, is in order. We translate, making
willgebroðor parallel with *dædfruman*:

> Books tell us
> how the first doers of men produced
> wealth and nourishment, the brothers of the will.

This interpretation secures a smoother translation except

for the uncertain meaning in context of *willgebroðor*.
But the possibility of an alternative reading suggests
deliberate ambiguity, pointing toward a hidden meaning
elucidated in scriptural commentary—what, in terms of
the introductory phrase, "Books tell us."

Scriptural exegesis suggests that both interpretations
of the passage are justified. If Adam and Eve are to stand
as the subject in the first alternative interpretation, *welan*
and *wiste* and *willgebroðor* are parallel as compound
object of the verb, *stryndon*. This interpretation finds
support since Cain and Abel, characterized by the poet
as the *willgebroðor*, represent the two directions of man's
will on earth, toward earthly possession, *welan*, or to-
ward spiritual sustenance, *wiste*.[20] Cain's name, in fact,
was understood to mean "possession"—possession of the
goods of this world for their own sake; Abel was taken
as meaning grief—grief in this world because of longing
for the heavenly home. St. Augustine in his *City of God*
makes much of this primary distinction; he begins his
extended discussion of the significance of the story of
Cain and Abel, "Born first, therefore, was Cain from
these two parents of the human kind, pertaining to the
City of Men; Abel after, pertaining to the City of God." [21]
The image of the two brothers as representing the two
directions of man's will in the use of the things of this
world is developed with clarity in a commentary reported
in the *Glossa ordinaria:*

> Cain and Abel, born of one mother, are figures representing
> all men who are propagated in this life from the root of sin; and
> some are lovers of the terrestrial city and of deadly delights,

and great in them is the yearning for *possession;* these Cain represents, whose name means *possession.* The others are in search of the future city, and, mourning in the afflictions of this dwelling place, with their whole desire are seeking to go to future glory: these Abel represents, whose name means *grief.*[22]

Thus "the books tell us" that Adam and Eve, the first sinners, after their sin begot two sons in whom were symbolized the future divisions of the human will.

On the other hand, Cain and Abel are literally the first men to be described in the Bible as working in the world, so that they are well characterized as *dædfruman,* first-doers, whether of good or of evil. Furthermore they were understood in their works to have produced the different goods of earthly possession and of spiritual sustenance. Because of this difference in their works, God accepted Abel's sacrifice and rejected Cain's. In explaining God's refusal of Cain's sacrifice, Augustine makes the fundamental distinction between use and enjoyment: "The good use the world to the end that they may enjoy God; the evil to the contrary, wish to use God so that they may enjoy the world." [23] St. Augustine also shows that Cain and Abel, the brothers of the will, are the first of the two generations of men, the sons of Babylon and the sons of Jerusalem. The sons of God, of Jerusalem, have their wills turned toward God and use the goods of this world (*welan*) so that they may achieve spiritual nourishment (*wiste*). The sons of earth have their wills directed toward the enjoyment of earthly goods.[24] The ambiguity of lines 969-971 appears deliberate, in the manner suggested by Christian theory and practice. The double value of key words forces the reader to search for their underlying significance.

The symbolic meaning of the story of Cain and Abel is suggested by the poet not only in the introductory ambiguity discussed, but also in his handling of the biblical account of Cain and Abel (972-1049). He begins, for example, with a contrast between the occupations of the two brothers, phrased in such a way as strongly to suggest that Cain is symbolically connected with the sons of earth and Abel with the sons of God (972-974):

> Oðer his to eorðan   elnes tilode
> se wæs ærboren   oðer ahte heold
> fæder on fultum.

The one [Cain] for his glory tilled the earth/ who was first born. The other held the possession/ of his father in assistance [or, in assisting his father].

Cain's works are related to *eorðan*, to the earth; Abel's works are related to his father, that is, anagogically, to God. Furthermore, the poet's account represents a considerable modification and condensation of the biblical story. Many of the details of the biblical account are omitted, and, except for verses 4:6-7, the biblical text is not expanded. There is a consequent emphasis on the thematic contrast between the works of Cain and those of Abel. Particular emphasis is placed on the enormity of Cain's sin. Lines 987-1001, an expository addition to the biblical text, lament the consequences of Cain's sin,

figuratively imaged as branches of the tree of evil, rooted
in one sin:

> After the slaughter-blow woe was raised up
> the progeny of affliction. From that shoot
> evildoings grew, the longer the stronger,
> the grievous fruit. Spread wide
> over mankind the branches of sin.
> The evil twigs touched hard and sore
> the sons of men—they do so still.
> From that the broad leaves of each strife
> began to sprout. We may of that tale,
> slaughter-grim fate, in lamentation speak
> not causelessly. And grievously us she injured
> the noble woman through the first sin
> that against God ever man did
> dwelling on earth since Adam became
> from God's mouth blessed with a soul.

Literally, the descendants of Cain, born after his sins,
are a progeny of affliction, because they perished in the
Flood. Symbolically, they are children of affliction be-
cause they dwell in the City of Babylon, of which Cain
is the spiritual founder. In its moral significance Cain's
sin represents the earthly beginning of all mortal, Baby-
lonian sin, for Cain sinned, according to patristic inter-
pretation, without the provocation of Adam and Eve,
misled by himself alone. Moreover, his sin was the first
sin committed after the expulsion from Paradise and was
committed in spite of the promise of the Redemption.
It was considered to be related in kind to the Devil's sin
of tempting Adam and Eve to destruction. For, like
Cain, Satan committed murder "because he slew Adam
in Paradise, when he persuaded him to eat of the apple,

and reduced him from immortality to mortality; and because of this he slew the race of men until the coming of the Saviour." [25] Although God expelled man from Paradise, He gave tokens of the Redemption, and in obedience to God and in praise of Him man may find the path back. But Cain rejected God's promise and raised the progeny of affliction, likened to a tree whose spreading branches suggest the moral implication of Cain's sin for all of mankind.

From the figure of the tree the poet turns with apparent abruptness to lament the sin of Eve. The transition, however, is abrupt only on the surface; Cain's tree of evil symbolically has roots in Eve's sin. Eve bore Cain under the curse of God for her sin in eating the tree's forbidden fruit. Cain's sin is a child of the first sin, as it is itself the original deadly sin in the world of exile. In the poet's figure, Cain's sin is a twig of the tree of forbidden fruit, which man in his disobedience caused to be the tree of evil; and from the twig of Cain's sin was to sprout the vicious luxuriance of sinning man. The image employed by the poet is used in biblical commentary on the sin of Eve; for example, in the *Glossa ordinaria*, cited above: "Cain and Abel, born of one mother, are figures representing all men propagated in this life from the root of sin (*de radice peccati*)." Cain's sin, deriving from original sin, is rooted in the tree of evil; in turn, his sin is the stem from which sprout the sins of the world. As we have seen in considering Bede's *De die judicii*, considerable exegetical development was given to the figurative values of the tree; and this figurative development underlies the poet's particular amplification. Through this means he was enabled to suggest emphatically the theme of the Babylonian refusal to praise God. The tree he describes is the tree of evil that is often found illustrated in manuscripts, a tree whose leaves bend toward the ground. The poet describes the twigs as bending down to touch man with their corruption. The biblical story of Cain's slaughter of Abel the poet organizes thematically. It is introduced and concluded by passages that enforce the underlying relevance of the story to man's duty to God. The events selected for treatment are similarly designed.

With the account of God's punishment of Cain the poet returns to a complete paraphrase of the genealogy of Cain. He begins, however, with the addition of a brief, but nonetheless significant, comment on a portion of Genesis 4:17, "and Cain builded a city." This city, the poet says, was the first city ever built (1058-1060):

> þæt wæs under wolcnum   weallfæstenna
> ærest ealra   þara þe æðelingas
> sweordeberende   settan heton.

That city was under heaven of walled keeps/ the very first of those which warriors/ sword-bearing have had builded.

Here is reiterated Cain's symbolic meaning as the founder of the earthly city and the prototype of those who dwell in it. St. Augustine says, "The first founder of the earthly city was a fratricide: for [Cain] overcome by envy, slew his brother, a citizen of the eternal city, pilgrimaging on this earth." [26] Or, according to Bede, Cain and his progeny "constructed a city, because all

impious ones are founded upon this life, where they have
their treasures; the saints, in truth, are guests and pil-
grims. Whence Abel, like the pilgrim Christian people
on earth, founded no city; for supernal is the city of the
just." [27]

The genealogy of Cain is paraphrased in full because
it has important Christian significance. Cain's progeny,
including as it does Jubal and Tubal, the founders of the
refinements of civilization (1087-1089), symbolizes the
earthlings. The genealogy ends with Lamech, who re-
ports (Gen. 4:23) that he has slain an unnamed man.
The poet identifies the slain man as Cain (1093-1098):

> "Ic on morðor ofsloh minra sumne
> hyldemaga. Honda gewemde
> on Caines cwealme mine
> fylde mid folmum fæder Enoses
> ordbanan Abeles eorðan sealde
> wældreor weres . . ."

I murderously slew one of my/ nearest kinsmen. I stained my
hands/ in my murder of Cain/ felled with my fist the father
of Enos/ the first slayer of Abel,/ gave to the earth/ the blood
of a murdered man.

The source of the information given by the poet is again
the "books." Lamech says (Gen. 4:24), "If Cain shall
be avenged sevenfold, truly Lamech seventy and seven-
fold." God's threat of sevenfold punishment for slaying
Cain was understood by the Fathers to imply a prophecy
of the destruction of the impious progeny in the seventh
generation from Adam. According to Bede, however,
God is actually saying to Cain, "Not as you think, will

you die and receive death for a remedy; you will live even to the seventh generation, and you will suffer in the flame of conscience."²⁸ After this statement Bede repeats the genealogy of Cain, ending with Lamech, "who the seventh from Adam involuntarily slew Cain." But, like the guarding of the gate, the threat of sevenfold punishment for the slayer of Cain and the seventy-seven-fold punishment for Lamech have a meaning that is related to the promise of the Redemption. As the threat of sevenfold punishment signifies the punishments that befell Cain himself in his "wandering and flight," the seventy-sevenfold punishments for Lamech are connected, through number symbolism, historically with the fate of the descendants of Cain and prophetically (allegorically) with the promise of salvation; the punishment for Lamech thus symbolizes the kin of Cain:

> LXX and VII souls were brought forth of the stem of Cain, who were to perish in the Flood. . . . Spiritually, moreover, Lamech represents the human race, both struck down through the deceit of the ancient enemy in the first parent and striking himself down in the increase of daily sins, for which seventy and sevenfold punishment is given; because even to the coming of Christ, Who appeared in the world in the seventy and seventh generation, punishment for the first disobedience crushed the human race, until He in His Coming lifted the sins of the world, and having opened the gates of the heavenly kingdom through His Baptism and Passion, led us into the eternal life which we had lost in Adam. Then the punishment of Lamech ceased.²⁹

Lamech's slaughter of Cain, a fact added to the Bible in commentary, implies the great themes of the Fall and the Redemption, which the poet has already emphasized.

From the slaughter of Lamech (Gen. 4:24) the Vulgate turns to the subject of the begetting of Seth (Gen. 4:25), "Then Adam knew his wife, and begat a son and called his name, Seth, saying, God has granted me another seed for Abel whom Cain killed. He began to invoke the name of the Lord." This statement the poet amplifies (1104-1116),

> Then became to Adam in repayment for Abel
> a son in the home, another born,
> a righteous son whose name was Seth:
> he was blessed and became for his parents
> gracious as a comfort for his father and mother,
> Adam and Eve, was a repayment for Abel
> in the world. Then spoke out
> the first of mankind: "Me the Eternal gave
> a son Himself, the Wielder of Victories,
> Ancient of Life, in place of my love
> that Cain slew, and from me,
> with this son, took away sorrow,
> our Lord: to Him for this be thanks."

The poet stresses the statement that Seth is a blessed replacement for Abel, particularly in Adam's speech of thanks, itself considerably enlarged. He thus underlines the significance of the event and connects it unmistakably with the preceding account of the generation of Cain.

The connection made in the poem between Cain and his generation and Seth and his is also made by the commentators. Bede, for example, interprets Cain's fratricide as signifying, in addition to the meanings already

163

given, the Passion of Christ: as Cain led Abel forth to slaughter, "the Jewish people led forth the Lord outside His city of Jerusalem and crucified Him in the place of Calvary." [30] Similarly, Lamech's killing of Cain has symbolic reference to the Redemption: "When, however, Lamech signifies Christ, his killing of Cain prefigures the killing of the Devil." Seth has a similar figurative meaning: "Seth is interpreted as Resurrection, which is Christ." [31] Thus the slaying of Abel by Cain represents the Passion; the killing of Cain by Lamech, Christ's triumph over the Devil; and Seth's coming to take the place of Abel, the Resurrection: "Spiritually moreover, just as the killing of Abel by Cain signifies the Lord's Passion, Seth, born for Abel, signifies Christ's Resurrection from death." [32] The external narrative in Genesis, properly interpreted, was understood to reveal prophetically the spiritual narrative of the Redemption.

The speech of thanksgiving under discussion is phrased with deliberate ambiguity to suggest the exegetical interpretation of Seth's birth, with its symbolic relation to Cain's slaughter of Abel. The speech begins (1111-1113):

> "Me ece sealde
> sunu selfe   sigora waldend
> lifes aldor   on leofes stæl . . ."

Adam is, of course, giving thanks to the Lord for Seth; but even a straightforward reading of the lines suggests the symbolic meaning of God's gift to Adam of Seth:

To me the Eternal gave the Son Himself, the Ruler of Victories
the ancient of life in the place of the dear one.

164

The reference is clearly to the symbolic meaning of Seth as the Saviour, the Son of God Who gave Himself for mankind. The literal application of Adam's words to Seth is not brought out until the next phrase, "for him whom Cain slew." Only with this phrase in mind may we reconstruct the sentence to give its literal meaning: "To me the Eternal Himself gave a son." In dividing the phrase "Eternal Himself," the poet employs the standard rhetorical device of *tmesis* to lead the reader to a perception of symbolic meaning.

Omitting the first three verses of Genesis 5, which refer back to Adam, the poet passes directly to the account of the days of Adam and the generation of Seth, which he paraphrases in detail for the obvious reason that the generation of Seth is the necessary antithesis to the generation of Cain. Thus, Bede, speaking of the order of the narrative in Genesis, says that the Bible, "after it had recounted the destruction of the fratricide, Cain, and unfolded in turn his accursed generation unto the seventh generation, returned to expounding the restoration of the holy seed." [33] Significantly, of the generation of Seth until Noah, Enoch receives the fullest treatment. Particularly expanded (1197-1213) is the brief twenty-fourth verse from the fifth chapter of Genesis. As translated from the Vulgate it reads: "Enoch walked with God and was not visible because God bore him up." Patristic exegesis accords to Enoch a position of considerable symbolic importance, for, as Bede points out, Enoch was born in the seventh generation from Adam and represents the peace of the elect in heaven; he is in direct contrast to Lamech, seventh from Adam in the wicked generation, who signifies the punishment of the wicked.[34] Furthermore, the translation of Enoch into heaven, which the biblical verse in question was understood to describe, signifies, according to Bede, the Ascension of Christ.[35] The symbolic meaning of the story of Enoch continues the thematic story of the Redemption which underlies the Genesis story.

Genesis 6:1-4 now treats of the events leading up to the Flood: (1) the mating of the sons of God and the daughters of men; (2) God's cryptically worded speech of warning, "My spirit will not remain (*permanebit*) in man for eternity, because he is flesh: and his ways were one hundred and twenty years"; (3) the dwelling upon the earth of giants and mighty men. In patristic commentary much is made of these three details, as may be seen in Bede's condensed summary:

> In the sons of God, the seed of Seth is signified. The seed of Seth is not inappropriately called the Son of God, because for Abel he was born, toward whose gifts the Lord looked in favor. By the *daughters of men*, in truth, the daughters of the seed of Cain are understood, whose copulation with the seed of Seth is the cause of the Flood upon the earth. . . . Beautiful they are called, that is, pleasing to the senses. And God said, *My spirit will not remain in man*, that is . . . because men have a brittle substance, I will not forever be angered against them. . . . I shall not consign them to eternal punishment, but will restore what they have merited. The *giants* that are spoken of represent the great sins, for they were born in the greatness of sin. Where Scripture speaks of *famous men*, it is to be understood as if it had said *proud* or *strong*.[36]

166

The Caedmonian Genesis

The poet (1245-1269) considerably amplifies the biblical verses, and his amplification clearly reflects the ideas found in commentary: He distinguishes between the sons of God and the daughters of men, employing the exegetical distinction between the seed of Seth and the seed of Cain (1245-1252):

> Then still was the kin of Seth,
> of the beloved progenitor greatly in charity,
> dear to God and blessed in salvation
> until the sons of God began for brides
> among Cain's kin to seek,
> the accursed people, and among them chose wives
> against God's pleasure, among the sons of men,
> maidens of the guilty ones, beautiful and fair.

The poet's handling of God's speech of warning seems also to reflect the exegetical interpretation of the somewhat cryptic biblical phrasing (1253-1262):

> Then spoke the Ruler of heavens,
> wrathful with mankind, and spoke these words:
> "These men have not from me in thought been parted,
> the tribe of Cain, but that kin
> has sorely angered me. Now the sons of Seth
> renew sorrow for me and to them take
> maidens for wives of mine enemies:
> there the beauty of women has sharply invaded,
> the loveliness of women and the ancient enemy,
> this tribe of men who were erewhile in peace."

What God means in saying, as the poet has it, "These men have not from me in thought been parted," is ambiguous until reference is made to biblical commentary. There God's speech is interpreted to indicate His clemency and His understanding of the weakness of man's flesh, so that "These men have not been parted from me in thought" means simply, "I have been deeply mindful of them." Biblical exegesis also helps to explain the connection of ideas in the line "the loveliness of women and the ancient enemy," for commentary explains the biblical "beauty of the daughters of men" as representing the beauty of the flesh that is "pleasing to the senses." Furthermore, the poet suggests the theme of the Fall by speaking of man renewing God's grief through woman and the Devil.

Biblical commentary is also reflected in the succeeding lines of the poem (1263-1269):

> Thereafter an hundred and twenty numbered count
> of winters in the world busied themselves in evil
> that damned folk until the Lord would
> on those faithless ones visit punishment
> and in death slay the guilty in deeds,
> the giant progeny unbeloved by God,
> the mighty evildoers hateful to God.

The lines reflect not only the exegetical significance of the giants and mighty men as sinners and enemies of God, but also the interpretation of "and his days will be one hundred and twenty years" as indicating God's clemency in allowing this time to sinners "for doing penance." [87] The kin of Cain did not repent but "busied themselves in evil." Like their progenitor, they flouted the possibility of redemption and in so doing called vengeance upon themselves. The time of the Flood is announced.

The central action of the ensuing biblical narrative is the building of the ark. This subject the commentaries treat in detail, with loving attention, since the ark was understood to symbolize the Church, and Noah, Christ.[88] In contrast, the poet omits almost all detail, perhaps because to suggest the fullness of commentary would have been to obscure structural emphasis on the themes of damnation and salvation. To support this is the fact that although the biblical narrative of the building of the ark is condensed, one brief addition is made which has the effect of emphasizing man's willful rejection of salvation. The addition (1317-1319) pictures Noah making a final attempt to warn his fellow men:

> He said to his kinsmen
> that a terrible thing was upon the people,
> fearful punishment. They recked not of this.

Similarly, although many details about the construction of the ark have been omitted, a concluding explanatory comment about the ark is added (1324):

> That is a wondrous kind:
> ever is it the harder when rough waters,
> the dark sea-streams, stronger beat.

The mysterious strength of the ark, a detail that is not in the biblical narrative, seems to echo the commentary. Bede, for example, says of the ark, that is, the Church, "Waves of tribulation frequently are bearing against it; the more vehemently they fill all things, the higher they compel her to seek the joys of the other life."[39] The poet, by employing the same figure, economically sug-

169

gests the commonplace interpretation of the ark as the
Church, the vehicle by which man may find the road
back. But the strength of the ark serves also to emphasize
the universal terror of the Flood, which sweeps over
those who refuse to heed Noah's warning.

The biblical description of the Flood (Gen. 7:17-23;
here translated literally from the OE of Aelfric) is brief:

> Was then a great flood become and the waters were mani-
> fold and they raised up the ark on high from the earth.
> And they rushed quickly and filled all the surface of the
> earth; truly the ark was borne over the waters.
> And the waters grew great over the earth; the highest moun-
> tains under all the heavens were concealed.
> The waters were fifteen cubits deep over the highest hills.
> And all flesh was destroyed which moved upon the earth:
> men, birds, beasts, reptiles.
> Each thing which had life was destroyed in the Flood.
> Except for those alone who were within the ark.[40]

From these details the poet has constructed an impres-
sive and significant description (1371-1406):

> The Lord sent
> rain from the heavens and also permitted broadly
> the fountains to oppress the earth,
> from each stream the flood waters
> black to roar. The seas rose up
> over the shore walls. Strong He was and terrible
> Who wielded the waters: He overwhelmed and covered
> the sin-guilty sons of the middle-earth
> with the dark waters, the dwelling-land of men
> and his homes He destroyed; mortal sins He avenged,
> God on men. The sea terribly seized
> upon the damned folk forty days
> and nights as well: enmity was fierce,

slaughter-grim for men. The King of Glory's
waves drove the life of the graceless
from their bodies. The Flood overwhelmed all,
rough under the heaven, the high hills
over the surface of the earth, and raised afloat
the ark from the earth and the noble people on it
whom He had blessed, the Lord Himself,
Our Creator, when He had sealed that ship.
Thereafter rode widely under the skies
over the back of the sea the best house,
proceeded with its burden. Upon the ship might not,
upon its passengers, the terrors of water
seize with violence, but them the Holy God
bore up and protected. Stood
deep over the hills the Flood,
fifteen cubits. That is a notable fate.
To these at the last was nothing as a portion,
unless she was raised up on the high heaven,
when the ocean army the progeny of earth
entirely destroyed, unless that ship-board,
the joy of angels had supported when Holy God
eternally above had permitted him, the renewed in spirit,
to mount the stream, the stern-hearted King.

The effect of the poet's amplification of the biblical narrative is to suggest the underlying meaning that was assigned to the Flood in scriptural commentary. The core of this meaning is given succinctly by Aelfric:

Noah, who was on the ark in that great Flood which drowned all the world except for these eight persons is rightly called *requies*, that is in English, *rest*; and he betokened Christ Who for this came to us, that He might have brought us from the waves of this world to rest and to bliss with Him.[41]

Further symbolic details, which make definite the mean-

ing of Noah as Christ and the riding of the ark on the
waters as salvation, are to be found in Bede's *Hexameron:*

> And the waters of baptism and faith, multiplied through the
> universal globe, raise up the Church from the lust for ter-
> restrial things to the hope and desire for heavenly life; but
> also the waves of tribulation are frequently beating upon the
> Church; so much the more vehemently they fill all, so much
> the higher they drive her to seek the joys of the other life.
> . . . The mountains signify the proud who raise themselves
> up in the glory of this world: whom the mountains of water,
> as it were, cover, but in these very same waters the ark is borne
> up because the flood of temptations overwhelms and swallows
> the proud and impious, but that same flood is overcome by the
> just, who in the free voyage of good works and of the winged
> mind fail not to move toward the port of eternal salvation.
> . . . Again the waters of the Flood raise up the ark on high
> and cover and hide the mountains because the sacrament of
> baptism by which the Church is raised up pushes down the
> high pride of the world and shows that it has nothing. And
> because we are baptized in the hope of future rest of soul and
> resurrection of the body in eternal life, which the wisdom of
> the flesh does not know, rightly is added: *Fifteen cubits deep
> was the water over the mountains which it covered.* Seven,
> indeed, and eight make fifteen; seven pertains to the rest of
> souls in the future after death because truly the Lord on the
> seventh of Sabbath lay still in the sepulchre; and, because, in
> truth, after the Sabbath, that is, on the eighth day, He arose
> from the dead, eight most fittingly signifies the time of our
> resurrection.[42]

Against such background the poet developed his descrip-
tion of the Flood. The central contrast in Bede's com-
mentary between the damned and the saved is reflected
in the poet's amplification that begins with the theme
of God's vengeance on the sinners and ends on the theme

172

of His mercy to the blessed. Specifically, Bede's commentary makes it possible to interpret a passage (1400-1406) that has occasioned much editorial difficulty, particularly in the following ambiguously phrased verses (1400-1401):

> þam æt niehstan wæs nan to gedale
> nymþe heo wæs ahafen on þa hean lyft.

The reference of the pronoun *heo* (she) has seemed sufficiently unclear to warrant emendation to *heof* (lamentation).[43] The difficulty disappears when we understand that the ark, the "she" of line 1401, is a primary symbol for the Church in its function of ministering God's redeeming Grace. Except in the ark—that is, the Church—as a true son of Noah, symbolically Christ, man may not avoid destruction and be lifted to salvation. Quite literally, as the poet phrases it, there is nothing for man unless she, the ark, is raised up on the waters of baptism. As Bede puts it in his *Pentateuch,* "Outside the ark, in truth, no flesh may be saved." [44] Similar difficulties in the remaining lines of the passage are resolved, since they serve simply to amplify this same basic idea: all are lost if God does not permit the ark to ascend, that is, the renewed in spirit within the Church to come to eternal rest.[45] The poet's purpose in amplifying the biblical description of the Flood was thematic: He wished to develop the contrasting themes of damnation and salvation, as reflecting God's might and man's need to praise Him.

The poet's description of the journey of the ark on the

waters is, for the most part, free paraphrase of the biblical text, with the very notable exception of his description of Noah's sending forth of ravens and doves to determine whether he could disembark. Certain details added by the poet are clearly of exegetical origin. But, of even greater significance, the underlying meaning of the biblical account reveals what thematic considerations led the poet to develop and elaborate this particular episode of the story of the Flood.

Noah dwelling in the ark symbolizes each of the blessed who "yearn toward rest in constancy of thought fixed on God," as the resting of the ark on the mountain signifies the time when a man whose heart and mind is fixed on God, "leading his life in pilgrimage, approaches in spirit the celestial joys." [46] This yearning of the souls within the ark to reach their resting place is well described by the poet in lines which have no counterpart in the biblical text (1431-1435):

> The men desired,
> the sea voyagers, and their wives also,
> the time they from the narrow place over the nailed sides
> might step upon the shore
> and from prison lead out their possessions.

The lines suggest that the ark is moving toward the harbor of heavenly rest, and they give the key to the ensuing description of Noah's sending forth of the birds. The actions of the birds in returning to the ark or in not returning were taken to signify types of man's Fall or Redemption in the pilgrimage of life.

The raven, which Noah first sent forth, did not return

to the ark. His failure to return is left unexplained in the Bible but is explained by Bede, who says that perhaps the raven did not return because it "had seized upon some dead body floating on the waters." [47] The poet has used the exegetical explanation of the conduct of the raven. Noah, the poet says, expected that if the raven found no dry land he would return to the ark, but (1446-1448),

> Yet his hope belied him
> and the enemy perched on the floating corpses:
> the dark-feathered one would not seek to return.

The raven is called by the poet "the enemy," for obvious symbolic reasons: The raven represents those who dwell in Babylon, the enemies of God, and those who refuse the way of Redemption, which leads to Jerusalem. Bede calls them "men most abominable in the shamelessness of their cupidity, devoted to the world." [48]

The doves Noah sends forth, to the contrary, represent various truths about the spiritual pilgrims in the ark. The first dove, "which, not finding rest, returned, shows that rest is not promised to the saints in this world." The dove that returned with the olive branch signifies those who, "though baptized outside the Church, if in them there is no lack of the oil of charity, may in after time be brought into unity." The third dove symbolizes the perfected man who has reached the ever-green harbor at the end of his pilgrimage "in the perfection of eternal salvation." [49] These flights are effectively and elaborately described by the poet, but the flight of the last dove is given symbolic meaning (1476-1482):

> Then once more the blessed man
> after a week the third wild dove
> alone he sent forth: she came not back
> flying to the ship, but land she gained,
> green woods: glad she would not ever
> under the dark roof again appear,
> on the board-fast ship—to her then was there no need.

Unlike the raven, who chose Babylon and lost forever his citizenship in his native land, the third dove found her home and had no need ever to return to the prison house.

The development given to the biblical narrative did not result from the promptings of the "Celtic spirit" or from the Anglo-Saxon inability to leave simplicity unadorned. Rather its purpose is to suggest the underlying meaning of the Flood that is particularly appropriate to the main theme of the poem, man's need to praise God, Whose might is revealed in the legend of salvation and damnation.

For the remainder of Noah's story the poet does not much elaborate the biblical text, except for a comment on the nakedness of Noah. God clothed Adam and Eve, and shame, says the poet, has become fitting to man (1565-1567),

> Since the Thane of Glory
> to our father and mother with fiery sword
> closed the native land of life.

The phrasing of the poet's commentary on Noah's nakedness recalls the important thematic symbol of the guarding of the gate of Paradise, with its dual significance of Fall and Redemption.

176

The *Caedmonian* Genesis

On the other hand, the poet handles the biblical gene-
alogies of the sons of Noah very freely, condensing, mod-
ifying, and amplifying them. What the poet does is to
select from the many names in Genesis 10, certain names
for special mention, while omitting any mention of most
of the names. For example, where Scripture merely men-
tions Japheth, the poet, though briefly and formally,
speaks of his reign and death (1604-1610). Yet of the
many descendants of Japheth he mentions only Geomor,
of whom the poet says, without biblical authority, that
he "dispensed his father's treasure among friends and
kinsmen" (1611). Such freedom of treatment contrasts
sharply with the detailed coverage of the earlier gene-
alogies of the descendants of Cain and Seth. These de-
scendants are covered in detail, presumably because of
the symbolic import of the two generations, the one of
Babylon, the other of Jerusalem. The descendants of the
sons of Noah have a more literal significance as the pro-
genitors of the various nations that peopled the earth,
but such historical significance seems not to have been
part of the poet's purpose. His selective treatment of the
sons of Noah is thematic and may be explained by refer-
ence to biblical commentary.

The poet begins with a formal account, without sug-
gestion from the biblical text, of the "reign and death of
Japheth" and of the succession of his son, Geomor, to dis-
pense "his father's treasure among friends and kinsmen"
(1604-1614). But after his elaborate beginning the poet
makes no mention of the other sons of Japheth or of their
descendants (Gen. 10:2-5). The poet's purpose, which

177

is clearly anything but genealogical, appears clearly from his subsequent treatment of the descendants of Cham. Of the numerous names given in Scripture, three only are given in the poem. Of these three, Chanan receives only mention, but Chus and his son, Nimrod, are in lines 1619-1636 given development comparable to that accorded to Japheth and Geomor. Chus, according to the poet, ruled righteously, but his son, Nimrod, who was of great might, was the first of the wicked kings of Babylon. The prominence thus accorded Nimrod in the poem is perhaps explained by Bede's remarks on Nimrod. Nimrod, the descendant of Cham, stands in contrast to the early descendants of Shem and Japheth: "While the progeny of Shem and Japheth remained in the innocence of the simple life, a cursed one was born of the stock of Cham, who perverted the status of human intercourse into a new kind of social living." Nimrod became the first tyrant; "gathering an army, he studied to exercise unnatural tyranny on the people." Spiritually, he was of the generation of the unjust, "neglecting heavenly things in which the just are strong to seek the baser things." As King of Babylon he represents, indeed, the devil himself: "For as Babel means *confusion;* rightly the founder of this, the head of all evils, declares himself figuratively as the devil." [50] As Cain is in spirit the ultimate human founder of Babylon, the city of the world, Nimrod is its actual founder, the first after the Flood to rule in the love of the world. In Nimrod is first fulfilled the curse pronounced by Noah (Gen. 9:25) against Cham for viewing in derision his nakedness, so that the emphasis given by

the poet to this earlier scene helps to prepare for the later
selective emphasis on Nimrod. It is specifically Nimrod's
Babylonian import that the poet stresses, for he signifi-
cantly omits any mention of Nimrod's famous role as
hunter (Gen. 10:9). Further to indicate the importance
of Nimrod, the poet employs the formula "books say"
in his description of him (1628-1635):

> A first-born then
> son of Chus wielded the treasure-throne,
> a famed man. Indeed writings tell us
> that he of mankind had most
> in that time might and strength:
> he was Babylon's first ruler,
> first of the nobles he raised up the native land's glory,
> increased and lifted it up.

Nimrod, King of Babylon, rules and conquers for the sake
of earthly glory, and he stands in unnatural contrast both
to his father, Chus, who ruled his kingdom wisely (1619-
1628), and to Geomor, who succeeded his father as a
true ruler (1604-1614). For Japheth ruled righteously
and his people prospered (1606-1610):

> He was himself blessed,
> mighty he maintained the blessings of his native land,
> prosperity among his children until his breast's treasure,
> his soul ready for death was appointed to go
> to the judgment of God.

Geomor continued the same orderly rule, without seeking
conquest or glory (1610-1612):

> Geomor thereafter
> the riches of the home apportioned to friends,
> to retainers and kinsmen, the son of Japheth.

By thus singling out from the genealogies the successions of Japheth-Geomor, Chus-Nimrod, the poet gives emphasis to the underlying thematic contrast between the two generations: the generation of Seth, which seeks redemption, is characterized by the peaceful rule of Japheth and the steady continuance in good of the son, Geomor; the generation of Cain, which rejects salvation, is characterized by the unnatural succession of Nimrod, King of Babylon, to the throne of the good king, his father.

The generation of Shem is not, like Cham's, accursed. Shem and Japheth share a true brotherhood in God. This brotherhood of piety is signalized for Bede in Genesis 10:21, the first verse of the account of the generation of Shem (10:21-31): "To Shem, the father of all the sons of Heber, the older brother of Japheth, were children born." Bede notes that Scripture "calls Shem the brother of Japheth but does not call him the brother of Cham." The omission, according to Bede, is deliberate, for Scripture "recognizes as true brothers those living singlemindedly in the faith of piety." More than this, the verse specially indicates the spirituality of Shem's generation in calling him "the father of all the sons of Heber," because this progeny followed the faith and piety "which through Heber descended to Abraham and the people of the Hebrews." [51] Heber is the direct opposite of the tyrannous Nimrod, the "author of the building of the tower, who against his nature strove to penetrate the heights of heaven." [52] The poet's treatment of the generation of Shem is designed to suggest this aspect of its general significance. For of the generation of Shem the poet mentions only Heber (1644-1648):

> In that progeny were men blessed
> of whom one was called Heber,
> descendant of Shem: from that noble arose
> a numberless people whom now all warriors
> and all earthdwellers call Hebrews.

The selection of Heber to represent the generation of Shem, which is called "blessed," and the emphasis given to Heber's founding the tribe of the faithful Hebrews show how the poet has seized on precisely the details which through biblical commentary have relation to the theme he is developing. For the generation of Shem is symbolized in Heber, the preserver and founder of the faithful tribe of "pilgrimage." Through the symbolic figure of Heber, the generation of Shem is connected with the good generation of Japheth and contrasted with the accursed generation of Cham, symbolized in Nimrod, King of the City of the World.

The thematic contrast between Heber and Nimrod also explains a minor but somewhat puzzling change in order found in the poem. In the Bible Nimrod is described in 10:8-10. There follow verses 10:11-32, which deal in part with the generation of Shem, including that of Heber. Then the next chapter begins with the verse "And the whole earth was then of one language." This verse was closely paraphrased by the poet (1635-1636):

> Reord was þa gieta
> eorðbuendum an gemæne

But he transposed it to a position immediately after his account of Nimrod and before the account of Heber. Apparently the poet transposed this verse to achieve a sharp contrast between Nimrod and Heber. For in patristic commentary it was Nimrod who was responsible for building the Tower of Babel and Heber, his contemporary, who retained the original language of the Faith. In shifting the line the poet calls attention to the fact that until the coming of Nimrod and his worldly pride the world spoke with the tongue of Adam, the tongue which Heber was still to keep. As Bede explains,

> This city in which the languages are separate and the people scattered is called Babylon, that is, *Confusion;* the other is called Jerusalem, that is, the *Vision of Peace,* in which concord is achieved, with the languages of all races united in the praise of God.[53]

In their contrasting use of speech Nimrod and Heber represent the two generations, the one which praises God and the other which praises the world. The change in the order of the verse emphasizes the difference between Nimrod and Heber.

Omitting, as we have seen, all mention of the other members of the generation of Shem (10:22-32), the poet passes from the notice of Heber to an amplification of Genesis 11:2. This amplification, in lines 1649-1660, is used by the poet as a formal introduction to his very free account (1661-1701) of the building of the Tower of Babel (11:3-8). In this sequence of events, which follows from his transposition of 11:1, the poet was not without authority. For the tenth chapter in Bede's *Penta-teuch* ends with a discussion of Nimrod's building of the tower, and the eleventh chapter begins with a commentary not on 11:1 but on 11:2, which concerns the moving of the people from the east into the land of Sennar. This commentary serves, as in the poem, to introduce a discussion of the significance of the Tower of Babel, for which discussion Bede reserved his commentary upon Heber, the preserver of the true tongue. In effect, both poem and commentary, by transposition of material, have concentrated attention on the contrast between Heber and Nimrod.

According to verse 11:2 the people went from the east, which signifies for Bede that "they retreated from the true light." Having retreated from the light, the sons of earth built the tower, which signifies, Bede continues, "the pride of this world or the impious dogmas of heretics." When they had fallen from the light and striven to demonstrate their pride in the world through the tower, the sons of earth became "divided from one another through the diversities of error," the spiritual state symbolized by the confusion of tongues.[54]

The underlying meaning of the going from the east in relation to the building of the tower is effectively suggested by the poet in the lines that begin the description of the migration (1649-1651):

> They proceeded from the east to lead their possessions,
> goods and cattle. The folk was single in mind,
> the strong warriors sought a wider land.

The amplification of the simple biblical statement "they fared from the east" by the addition of the phrases having to do with possessions emphasizes the attention of the evil ones to worldly goods, which is the implicit cause for their "retreat from the light." Chrysostom's explanation is standard: The sons of the earth are moved by restless dissatisfaction so that they "cannot live within prescribed limits, but desiring more, always long for even greater things." [55] They turn their backs on the east, Paradise, which shines in God's light, in their desire for worldly goods. This folk is, according to the poet, *anmod*, a word which is found elsewhere in OE poetry always applied to evildoers or non-Christians preparing for some act, whether good or bad. [56] The word thus suggests that the folk is evil and, with the accompanying emphasis on possessions, further suggests that it is preparing to act evilly.

In this search for earthly goods, "they came to a plain in the land of Sennar, and there they dwelled" (11:2). Ironically, Sennar means, as Bede explains, "gnashing of teeth" or, alternatively, "stench." In turning from the east to Sennar in the hope of earthly happiness the evil people have in actuality found the exterior darkness:

> What by the land of Sennar is meant but the stinking lust of carnal folly? Whoever do not shun dwelling there, with fixed and resolute intention, soon with increasing evil, invite their neighbors to injustice against the Creator and to evil deeds. [57]

The deceptiveness of settling in Sennar is effectively suggested by the poet (1655-1660):

They settled Sennar wide and far,
the leaders of the people with dear men,
in the days of their years, the green fields,
the fair earth. To them continuing
in the space of their days were riches
according to their desire of each growing success.

They have found, that is, the grass of which Gregory
speaks, growing in the shade of the world and withering
in the sun of God, the grass of earthly glory, growing
brightly in its season and then passing into dust.[58] They
have amassed the earthly treasure which gives only the
dissatisfaction of increased desire.

The meaning of the building of the tower has already
been suggested. Indeed, since its symbolic import is
suggested by the biblical text itself, the poet is content
with simple changes for clarity and dramatic effective-
ness. For example, in line 1668 he adds to the biblical
text the reason for building the tower, *þæs þe hie gesoh-
ton Sennera feld,* "as a sign that they had sought the
field of Sennar." The addition reminds the reader of the
causal connection between the journey from the east and
the building of the tower. The poet (1672-1674) makes
clear by choice of the words the wrongfulness of the
building. They sought

> men for the work and the evil making
> until for pride and darkness of mind
> they made known their strength.

The work is "beyond the scope of man" (*ofer manna
gemet*), line 1677. Finally, to the spare biblical account
of the confusion of tongues, with its important symbolic

meaning, the poet adds a vigorously realistic picture (1687-1696) of the plight of the workmen when they found they could no longer communicate one with the other.

After the account of the Tower of Babel, Genesis 11:10-28 repeats in fuller detail the generation of Shem, culminating in the birth of Abraham, whose life becomes the subject of the immediately ensuing chapters. This long genealogical account, in verses 11:10-25, is briefly summarized by the poet in lines 1702-1711. Of the descendants of Shem the poet mentions only the father of Abraham and Aaron. He concludes (1710-1711) with special mention of God's particular care of these two:

> þam eorlum wæs
> frea engla bam   freond and aldor

To these men was/ the joy of angels, to both, friend and leader.

In further contrast to the summarizing account of the preceding generations of Shem, the poet paraphrases carefully the biblical account of the birth of Aaron's son, Lot, and adds special mention of the continuing service to God of the kinsmen, Abraham and Lot (1714-1718):

> These kinsmen throve before the Lord,
> Abraham and Lot, blessedly
> as to them from their forefathers was their
>   noble nature
> in the kingdom of the world: therefore widely
>   now they
> are celebrated for their noble deeds among
>   the sons of the people.[59]

By omitting the details of the generation of Shem and thus emphatically introducing the figure of Abraham, the poet connects closely the kinsmen Abraham and Lot with Heber and the generation of the faithful, as against Nimrod and the generation of the faithless. Abraham and Lot continued in the righteous ways of their ancestors; Nimrod and his followers fell into Babylonian error and diversity of tongues. True descendants of Heber, Abraham and Lot continued to dwell, says Augustine, "in the one house where the true God alone is worshipped . . . and where the Hebrew tongue alone remained." In this house, "the garden of the City of God is kept, as in Sennar is kept the field of the Earthly City." [60] Augustine makes a further general contrast of the two cities:

> True piety alone remained in those generations which descended from the seed of Shem, through Arphaxat, and continued to Abraham: but from that pride of building a tower to the skies, in which impious self-exaltation is signified, became visible the city, that is, the society of the unjust. [61]

Augustine's comment is reflected in the modifications made by the poet.

In addition, the poet's emphasis in introducing Abraham serves to mark the transition to the next large episode in the underlying spiritual drama which the poet seems to be suggesting behind the surface of the biblical story. In the building of the tower Augustine saw "the City of the Unjust made visible," in the story of Abraham, "the first manifestations of the City of God." Nimrod and his followers symbolize the falling away from God of the children of the earth; in Abraham is symbolized the regenerative power of faith. His story is symbolically the story of the road back, of Christ's Redemption; for, as Augustine says, in the time of Abraham not only "does the idea of the City begin to be apparent, but also the divine promises are read more clearly, which now in Christ we see fulfilled." [62] It is perhaps to indicate one of the most important of the "more clearly read" truths that the poet develops the biblical mention of Abraham's taking of a wife, Sarah (1719-1729). Sarah, "sterile in youth and fulfilled in age through the son of promise," typifies Holy Church. [63] To this symbolic meaning of Sarah the poet calls attention by employing the "books tell us" formula (1722-1723):

> Seo fæmne wæs
> Sarra haten   þæs þe us secgeað bec.

With this formal and symbolic introduction of Abraham and Sarah the poet turns to the story of Abraham, which, to the Sacrifice of Isaac, occupies the remainder of the poem.

The poet paraphrases the beginnings of the story to the separation of Abraham and Lot (11:31–13:4) in lines 1730-1890. The paraphrase is, as usual, free. The modifications and amplifications in general tend to suggest the special providence watching over Abraham, and Abraham's faith in God. Lines 1808-1813, for example, which have no counterpart in the biblical text, emphasize God's beneficence toward Abraham by calling attention to the reward God granted to Abraham for his sacrifice, so that Abraham enjoyed all good things. To emphasize

Abraham's faith the poet somewhat modifies the story of the way in which Abraham avoids danger by having Sarah say to the Egyptians that she is his sister (12:13): "Say now, I beg you, that you are my sister, so that it will be well to me through you, and my soul will live through your grace." Abraham's request is considerably softened in the poem through what the poet adds to the biblical text (1837-1843):

> So you shall my
> life protect, if the Lord to me protection,
> in His earthly Kingdom the Ruler,
> the Almighty, will grant as He did before,
> longer life, Who for us this path created
> that we among the Egyptians should grace,
> comfort, and safety desire to seek.

What in the biblical text seems, if not cowardly, at least overcautious, in the poet's version becomes an example of Abraham's faith and trust in God, to Whom he committed, as Bede explains, "the protection of his wife, as a man bewaring human treacheries, because if he had not avoided the danger in so far as he was able, he would rather have been putting God to test than trusting in Him." [64]

The ensuing story of the separation of Lot and Abraham (13:6-18) is paraphrased by the poet in lines 1890-1959. The paraphrase reveals some interesting amplifications and modifications. Genesis 13:8-9 recounts Abraham's speech in which, fearful of the discord that has arisen between Lot's shepherds and his own, Abraham counsels separation to avoid occasions of hate. As a glance at the text will indicate, the poet, in lines 1900-1919, has considerably amplified his speech, perhaps because the biblical speech was considered an important admonition to all men that they "should place nothing before charity and concord." [65] After they agree to separate, Lot chooses to dwell in the beautiful land of Sodom and Gomorrah, although the people there are evil (13: 11-13):

> Lot then chose for himself the earth about the Jordan and proceeded from the East, and they became divided each from his brother.
>
> Abraham lived in the land of Canaan. Lot truly dwelled in the cities which were about the Jordan and he lived in Sodom.
>
> The men of Sodom were most wicked and very sinful before the Lord.

To his paraphrase of these verses (1920-1936) the poet adds a commentary (1937-1944):

> Never would
> Lot adopt the customs of those people
> but fled the evil habits of that nation
> although in that land he had to live—
> sin and evil—and he held himself fairly,
> faithful and guiltless in that people,
> even most like to one, mindful of teachings,
> who knew not what that progeny did.

This defense of Lot's intentions is also found in biblical exegesis. "It is tacitly added to the praises of the blessed Lot," says Bede, "that though living among the Sodomites" he could not be corrupted "through the riches or example of the neighboring people." [66]

The Caedmonian Genesis

The simple statement (13:12) that Abraham dwelled in Canaan appears in the Bible almost as part of the story of Lot. The poet shows his detailed concern for narrative order in introducing this statement in the poem only after completing his account of Lot, with its added commentary. Concerning Abraham, however, he does not attempt to go beyond the mere transposition and translation of the beginning of verse 12:

> Abraham wundode eðeleardum
> Cananea forð.

He fails entirely to translate or paraphrase 13:14-18, verses which recount God's promises to Abraham and Abraham's obedience to God. For this biblical account, on the other hand, the poet substitutes a passage of expository comment that simply affirms God's special care for Abraham (1946-1959):

> Him the King of Angels,
> the Lord of Mankind, held in protection,
> in pleasant fruits and the world's treasures,
> in love and delight. Therefore they say his praise
> widely under heaven, the progeny of men,
> the sons of baptism. He served his Joy,
> according to his [or His] pleasure in the native land
>   while he possessed the earth,   [1952]
> holy and wise in heart. Never lacking a protector
> in any way need be any
> living man, fearful and afraid,
> man before his God, a man who in return ever,
> through success of memory, in mind and deed,
> with word and thought, in wise thanks,
> in this bodily life will serve Him.

The simplest explanation for the poet's substitution of a passage of hortative generalization for the expected paraphrase of God's promises to Abraham is that in commentary the three promises were considered to have a single underlying meaning; thus, in place of a paraphrase, a generalization about the significance of the final promise could serve as summary, particularly since the first two promises had been fully paraphrased in lines 1744-1766 and 1784-1790. The promises were understood in their figurative sense, individually and collectively, to prophesy that from the seed of Abraham, the father of the faithful, would come Christ, whose act of Redemption would be operative for all mankind. The land God promised to Abraham and his seed was understood to represent, according to Bede, the "kingdom of the heavenly patria." In short, what God promised to Abraham is the Redemption. This figurative meaning of the promise is reflected in the passage.

The seed of Abraham are represented in the poem by the "sons of baptism" (*fullwona bearn*), for symbolically Abraham's seed, as Rabanus says, are those who "follow the footsteps of the faith." [67] The promise of the patria is perhaps suggested in the contrast between *eðle*, native land, and *eard*, earth, in line 1952:

> He frean hyrde
> estum on eðle   ðendum he eardes breac.

Abraham obeyed God with good will on earth [or, for the inheritance in the native land] while he enjoyed the earth.

The phrase with its semantic potentialities was perhaps

deliberately made ambiguous, as frequently in the poem, to suggest the underlying meaning. "The sons of baptism say Abraham's praise" because through Abraham God showed that no man need to be "fearful before Him" if he "will serve Him" as did Abraham, "in thought and deed," "in word and thought," "in wise thanks."

Particularly in these last lines of the passage the poet seems to reflect Bede's interpretation of God's third promise to Abraham, "All this land you see, I grant to you and your offspring in eternity" as representing "the heavenly patria." [68] The land promised by God was interpreted to mean heaven, partly because heaven is the reward of those who live in charity, and these were held to be symbolized in Abraham's sacrifice after the promise. Abraham's altar represents the human heart and his sacrifice represents prayer and good works:

> The fire of love, in which the chosen are kindled toward offering to God the sacrifice of prayer or good works, never fails on that altar, that is, in their hearts . . . because in this life they burn with divine love and in the future, seeing God, they will love Him more perfectly with their whole heart and soul and power.[69]

Bede's comment, like the poet's, shows how Abraham's actions teach the ideal of Christian conduct.

Moreover, in the substitution of general commentary for paraphrase, the poet may have had a larger structural purpose in mind. First, in the passage immediately following the one under discussion the poet employs a formula of epic poetry, "Ða ic aldor gefrægn Elimitarna" (Then I heard the Lord of the Elamites). The epic form-

ula of introduction strongly suggests the celebration
of warlike deeds, and, in fact, the poet does turn to the
activities of Abraham as a successful warrior. Thus, the
generalizing commentary seems to mark the close of a
section in the poetic life of Abraham, as the *gefrægn*
formula perhaps marks the beginning of the next section.
A possible basis for this division is to be found in Bede's
commentary on God's command to Abraham before His
first promise to him (12:1): "Go you from your land, and
your people and the house of your father." Abraham
in fulfilling this command serves as an example to us all
that if we are to be saved, we must go out

> *from our land,* that is, from the faculties of this earth; and
> *from our people,* from the habits and customs and the primal
> sins which are joined to us from birth as if through blood; and
> *from the home of our father,* that is, from the memory of all
> this world, as it were, from our kindred, so that having re-
> nounced we shall be able to spread among the people of God
> and be led to the land of the heavenly promise when the time
> has come.[70]

The three teachings contained in God's command are
called by Bede respectively the teachings "of a son, of a
man, and of a soldier." For the child must learn to leave
behind his instability, the man, "his sins, and the teach-
ing of the soldier is to leave behind the memory of this
world." [71] Expressed in a more familiar fashion, God
commands Abraham to conquer, in order, the world, the
flesh, and the Devil—through faith, which fixes the mind
on God, through hope, which leads man to live on the
true pilgrimage, through charity, which by the active

realization in good works of the love of God leads to a forgetting of the world. We have had exemplified the faith and hope of Abraham, which led him to be obedient to God in all things and to trust to Him in Egypt. We have had his charity foreshadowed in his decision to keep concord between himself and Lot. We shall now "hear" of warlike deeds, of the might of the kings of earth pitted against Abraham, the soldier of the Lord. In his struggle against the powers of the world, and particularly in his rescue of Lot from these powers, Abraham's charity will be demonstrated. The ensuing story of Abraham the warrior is highly amplified by the poet, who makes it almost into a set piece—in many ways the most dramatic in the poem. However, the poet's elaboration of the episode is less likely to be due to an effort to recall heroic glories in the midst of biblical paraphrase than to an effort to picture Abraham, the soldier of God, the symbol of charity.

Certainly on the surface the poet seems to linger with what must appear a very un-Christian delight in the heroics of battle and in poetic expression for its own sake. Because of the length of this battle narrative, which takes up lines 1960-2095, a summary must suffice. The story begins swiftly with an account of the attack by the four kings "from the north," as they are identified by the poet, on the five "southern kings" of Sodom and Gomorrah. The ensuing battle narrative is characteristically "heroic" in its combination of realistic detail and formal epithet. After the success of the northern kings, "many a fearful maiden," the poet says, "had trembling to go to a stranger's embrace" (1969-1971). Their defenders perish, "sick with wounds" (1972). After twelve years of paying tribute, the conquered people rebel (1976-1981). The four northern kings and the five southern kings again do battle; "the javelins sing, the raven croaks, greedy for prey," says the poet in the stock heroic phrases (1983-1985). The "battleplay" is hard, but the northern kings "possess the place of slaughter" (2005). Lot is among the captives of the victorious kings (2013-2017). A survivor escapes to Abraham (2018-2023). Abraham gathers a small band of 318 warriors to encounter the mighty northern host (2024-2052). He comforts his tiny band, declaring his faith that "the Eternal Lord might easily grant good speed in the spear strife" (2057-2059). In the ensuing battle, "Abraham gave war as a ransom for his nephew, not the wound gold" (2069-2070). Lot is freed; the bodies of the northern army are torn at by the carrion birds (2087-2089). The poet concludes (2092-2095):

> Næfre mon ealra
> lifigendra her   lytle werede
> þon wurðlicor   wigsið ateah,
> þara þe wið swa miclum   mægne geræsde.

Never any/ living man with a little band/ more worthily had engaged in battle,/ against so mighty a force struggled.

In these concluding words the poet seems to echo commentary: "A very great miracle indeed of the divine power is that Abraham, with so small a band, caused the overthrow of so great an enemy." [72]

The poet has, in short, written a traditional and highly

developed battle narrative, with some emphasis on Abraham's faith in God, but with little other obvious Christian motivation. Yet the poet's intention will be missed if patristic commentary is not considered; for there the battle between the five kings and the four was considered to be an important symbol of the conquest over the five senses, represented in the defeated kings, by four states of sinful living, represented in the four northern kings. The four states of sinful living, which conquer man through his senses, are heresy, heathen folly, hypocrisy, and avarice.[73] In turn, Abraham's battle against the four kings "signifies the battle of the virtues and the vices." It is, in short, the first *psychomachia*. The victory of Abraham's little band of 318 is made, through number symbolism, to represent the Redemption: "In this number is signified the sign of the most victorious cross and the name of our Saviour, Jesus Christ." [74] Abraham's victory is important because it exemplifies the symbolic victory of the Christian soldier over worldly temptation; in this victory Abraham shows how "our faith, the victor, triumphs in the soul over the exterior man." [75] The poet's vigorous battle scenes do not celebrate the memories of heathen poetry; rather symbolically they celebrate the triumph of the Christian soldier. The intended effect on the audience, as we may conjecture, was to arouse with dramatic immediacy and through the use of the ancient poetic idiom the remembrance of basic Christian doctrine. They were to see in Abraham not a pagan warrior, but an ideal of Christian living.

Although this meaning is not stated explicitly in the

course of the battle narrative, it is suggested by the poet in his ensuing amplification (2107-2119) of the words of Melchisedech to Abraham, in Genesis 14:18-19. Melchisedech appears only once in Genesis, but his mysterious figure is given importance by St. Paul's reference to him in Hebrews 7. Melchisedech was considered by the Fathers to represent Christ and the apostolic succession, the "evangelical pontificate," which is realized in Christ and, through Peter, is passed on to the bishops of the Church. This traditional symbolism explains the poet's epithet (2103) for Melchisedech, *leoda bisceop*, the bishop of the peoples, a phrase not suggested by the biblical text.[76] His speech to Abraham, in the poet's version, begins with an ambiguity (2107-2109):

> Wæs ðu gewurðod   on wera rime
> for þæs eagum   þe ðe æsca tir
> æt guðe forgeaf: þæt is god selfa.

You have been honored in the number of men/ before the eyes of Him Who to thee spear-glory/ in battle granted: that is, God Himself.

Abraham is honored in the number of men, that is, "among men," but also quite literally in the number, 318, of his little band, which symbolically was prophetic of the Redemption through which, as we have seen, the faithful Christian soldier everywhere triumphed: "In this number is signified the sign of the most victorious cross and the name of our Saviour, Jesus Christ." [77]

The King of Sodom addresses a simple request to Abraham in Genesis 14:21: "Give to me the living souls, the rest do you take." The poet expands this simple request into a plea of deliberate rhetorical artifice culminating effectively in the King's appeal to the pathos of his bereavement and worldly suffering (2133-2135):

> Eaforan syndon deade,
> folcgesiðas, nymðe fea ane,
> þe me mid sceoldon   mearce healdan.

Our sons are dead/ and the warriors few indeed/ who with me shall hold the marches.

Abraham's reply is of equal effectiveness, but its appeal is to eternal values. He will not take earthly treasures, he vows before God, lest it be said that he, through his battle, became wealthy in the earth's goods; but his warriors should receive their proper share. He ends with a grim word of comfort: the King has no longer any need to fear the men from the north (2159-2161):

> Ac nefuglas
> under beorhhleoþum   blodige sittað,
> þeodherga wæle   þicce gefylled.

But the gorged birds/ in the mountain retreats sit bloody,/ with the slain of the army tightly filled.

Abraham's answer to the King of Sodom, the biblical text of which the poet lovingly elaborates, is, according to Bede, "diligently to be observed," for it is "an example of the moral life." In fighting to free Lot, Abraham shows his love for his neighbor; in giving the tithe to Melchisedech, his devotion to God; in refusing the wealth of the King of Sodom, he shows himself "a despiser of earthly rewards"; in his care that his men receive their proper

deserts, he shows himself "a lover of justice."[78] Thus,
the apparent reason why the poet developed the episode
of Abraham's victory was in order to relate it, in its sym-
bolic meaning, to the theme of salvation. Abraham's
victory shows man how he may gain his eternal home
by leaving the world behind.

In contrast to the amplification of the account of Abra-
ham as soldier, the point of highest dramatic action, the
rest of the poem moves rather swiftly, and the scriptural
text is modified rather in the direction of condensation
than of amplification. For example, Genesis 15 is con-
cerned with Abraham's complaint to God that no son has
yet been given him (2-3); with God's reply (4-7); with
Abraham's elaborate preparations for divining accord-
ing to God's instructions (8-11); with a vision in which
Abraham hears God speak (12-21). In the poet's version
the action is simplified and condensed to a simple col-
loquy between God and Abraham in which the details
that occupy verses 8-17 are omitted. The effect of the
condensation is to emphasize God's repeated promise
that Abraham's descendants will be in number like the
stars—figuratively, a promise that all the "blessed and the
just," the redeemed, will be the spiritual descendants
of Abraham.[79] Furthermore, God's somewhat vaguely
phrased promise that Abraham will have an heir the poet
particularizes by an addition to the scriptural text (2197-
2200):

> Gien þe sunu weorðeð
> bearn of bryde þurh gebyrd cumen
> se ðe æfter bið yrfes hyrde,
> gode mære.

Yet to you will a son,/ child of the wife through birth, come/ who, after you, will be protector of the inheritance,/ illustrious in good [*or* in God].

The wordplay, *bryde* and *gebyrd,* seems deliberate. The same wordplay is found, for instance, in the Exeter *Christ* I, line 38, with reference to the Immaculate Conception. The son promised by God to Abraham is Isaac, who prefigures Christ. God's promise that the sterile Sarah in her old age will give birth is prophetic of the Immaculate Conception and of the coming of the Redeemer.[80]

The story of the birth of Ishmael is told without much variation from the biblical text. But in his paraphrase of Genesis 17 the poet omits verses 3-9, part of God's speech to Abraham. The verses contain general promises of the spread of Abraham's seed. The function of the omission is to give increased emphasis to God's direct promise (17:16, 19) that Sarah, Abraham's wife, will bear a child, Isaac (2327-2332):

> þu scealt sunu agan
> bearn be bryde þinre   þone sculon burhsittende
> ealle Isaac hatan.   Ne þearf þe þæs eaforan sceomigan
> ac ic þam magorince   mine sylle
> godcunde gife   gastes mihtum,
> freondsped fremum.

Thou shalt possess a son,/ child by thy wife whom those dwelling in cities will/ call Isaac. Nor need you be ashamed of this child,/ but I to that good warrior shall give/ my godly gift [*or* love, a godly gift] through might of the spirit/ good friendspeed.[81]

What the passage suggests is that Isaac, as a son born to

a sterile woman and a very old man, is a special indication of God's grace. In place of the biblical introduction of the name Isaac (17:19), "You will call him Isaac," the poet has given the formal statement, "whom those dwelling in cities will call Isaac." The generalized form of this statement, along with the poet's use of the otherwise unrecorded *freondsped,* multitude of friends (?), perhaps suggests Bede's comment that God's promise concerning Isaac is prophetic "of the calling of the nations" to salvation, through the abounding grace of God.[82]

The poet continues the biblical narrative with little modification until he comes to 19:24-25, which recounts the destruction of Sodom and Gomorrah. In lines 2545-2560 the poet considerably amplifies the simple biblical statement of destruction. The amplification serves a thematic purpose, since the destruction of the cities is said to signify "the torment of final punishment, when all the damned will be seized in the eternal fire." On the other hand, Lot's escape from that destruction symbolizes, like the birth of Isaac, the promise of the Redemption.[83] Particularly notable in the amplified description are lines 2550-2551:

> Lig eall fornam
> þæt he grenes fond goldburgum in.

The flame destroyed all/ that it found green in the golden city.

The flame destroys the transitory green of earthly show, which is the opposite of eternal green, symbolized in the Christmas tree; the green destroyed by the flame is that of the city of false gold, the opposite of the golden city of Jerusalem.[84] The poet also expands through commentary the succeeding verse: "And looking back, his wife was turned into a pillar of salt." He begins his amplification with the formula "writings tell us" (2565-2575):

> Writings tell us
> that she soon became in a salt stone's
> likeness: ever thereafter
> the image—that is a famous story—
> remained in silence where she was visited
>   with the dire
> punishment because the words of the servants
>   of glory she
> would not heed. Now hard and towering she must
> in that place await her fate,
> the judgment of the Lord, until the number and
> the world of days shall pass—that is one
>   of the wonders
> which the Ancient of Glory has made.

The pillar of salt was literally one of the wonders of God's creation, for as Bede explains, "Josephus reports that even in his day the same statue of salt endured at the gates of that same city." Symbolically, Lot's wife represents those who, "renouncing the world, and beginning on the hard road of virtue, unstable and like a woman at heart, suddenly turn back to those desires for the world which they had left," [85] and the warning she conveys to those who would be saved is given special prominence by Christ Himself, Who said (Luke 17:32), "Be ye mindful of Lot's wife." In these words, according to Bede in his commentary on Luke, Christ warns those who "in trouble look behind, and turn from the hope of the divine promise." [86] The fate of Lot's wife suggests the theme of damnation.

Further details of omissions and modifications are all minor, so that the problem posed by the ending of the poem as it appears in the Junius MS may now be considered. The poem, it will be recalled, paraphrases Genesis only through the account of Abraham's sacrificing, at God's behest, a ram in place of his son Isaac (22:13). The poem as it survives is concluded with five lines without counterpart in the biblical text (2932-2936):

> Abrægd þa mid þy bille, brynegield onhread,
> reccendne weg rommes blode,
> onbleot þæt lac gode, sægde leana þanc
> and ealra þara sælða þe him sið and ær,
> gifena drihten, forgifen hæfde.

He brandished his sword, prepared the burnt offering,/ the altar smoking with the blood of the ram,/ sacrificed that gift to God, said thanks for gifts,/ which He to him early and late, all those gifts the Lord had given him.

Although it is possible "that there is no telling how much more may have been contained in the poem as originally written, and how much may possibly have been lost," [87] it should be observed that the praise of Abraham for the gifts of God is in accord with, and thus structurally returns us to, the beginning of the poem, with its admonition that we praise God:

> Us is riht micel ðæt we rodera weard,
> wereda wuldorcining, wordum herigen,
> modum lufien.

This suggestion of thematic echo, along with the other evidence of deliberate thematic structure, encourages the belief that the poem is complete as it stands. It is at least questionable that the poem is incomplete in the manuscript because "the sequence of events follows the Old Testament narrative without deliberate reorganization or reconstruction of the material, and the plan of the poem permitted therefore the versification of the whole of the Genesis without violation of any artistic unity."[88] We have investigated the poem in sufficient detail to observe that it is far from a simple paraphrase of Genesis; indeed the modifications and alterations seem best explained on the grounds of a thematic purpose that perhaps would not have been served by a "versification of the whole of the Genesis."

The practice of the Latin Christian poets may suggest an answer; for example, we recall that there are various types of Genesis poems. There is a straight paraphrase like the *Heptateuchos*, attributed to a certain Cyprien;[89] on the other hand, there is the *Genesis* attributed to Hilary of Arles, which begins, as we have seen, very much in the manner of the *Genesis* A, "Dignus opus et justum semper tibi dicere grates." This brief poem is perhaps thematic in structure. It selects incidents from Genesis to show man that it is right and fitting that he praise God.[90] To serve this thematic purpose, Hilary's *Genesis* ends with the Flood. Similarly, the *Alethias*, attributed to Claudius Marius Victor, is a versified commentary and paraphrase but ends with the thoughts of judgment arising from the account of the destruction of

Sodom and Gomorrah.[91] Of apparent significance, in view
of the frequent parallels betwen Bede's *Hexameron* and
Genesis A, is the fact that Bede's commentary ends with
the childhood of Isaac, and it seems probable that both
Bede and the *Genesis* poet had a reason for ending with
Isaac. The reason is to be found in the ultimate under-
lying meaning of Genesis and the specific meaning of
Isaac. Honorius of Autun gives a succinct statement of
the meaning of Genesis: "Moses' intention is to tell fig-
uratively *the Redemption of the human race through
Christ,* to which intention he is willing in every way to
adapt his material." [92] Isaac, specifically in this general
plan, signified "the Saviour, Christ, Who died for us." [93]
In Isaac the prophetic promise of the Redemption is
completed. The poet could have found no more satis-
factory episode on which to end.

Genesis A seems not to be a mere paraphrase. It fol-
lows a plan in developing the related concepts of the Fall
and the Redemption, as they are prefigured in Genesis,
in order to enforce the basic theme announced at the be-
ginning of the poem—the praise of God. Beginning with
this theme, the poet shows the angels blissful in their
praise of the Creator and, in contrast, the bitter fate of
the fallen angels, who would not praise Him. He then
speaks of the creation of the world, which in God's inten-
tion will be populated by a race that may prove itself
worthy through obedience to inherit the empty thrones
of heaven. The interpolated *Genesis* B tells of the Fall of
Man. In the remaining portion of *Genesis* A are developed

those portions of the biblical story which trace figura-
tively the salvation and damnation of mankind, first sym-
bolized in the actions of expelling Adam and Eve from
Paradise. Cain's slaying of Abel symbolizes the results of
the Fall—man's self-willed sinning. On the other hand, the
slain Abel symbolizes the Redeemer and the Redemp-
tion. Cain builds the Earthly City, and his descendants
corrupt the children of God, so that He sends the Flood,
with its figurative picture of salvation and damnation.
After the account of the Flood, the poet contrasts Nim-
rod, King of Babylon, with the good progeny, particularly
Heber, the ancestor of Abraham. It is on Abraham, as a
figurative character, that the poet chiefly concentrates.
In Abraham, particularly in his victory over the world, is
reflected the way of the just man. In the fall of Sodom
and Gomorrah is symbolized both salvation, in Lot's
escape, and damnation, in the destruction of the city and
in the fate of Lot's wife. The sacrifice of Isaac represents
the fulfillment of God's promise to Abraham of the birth
of Christ and the Redemption of mankind. The poem
ends, as it began, in thanksgiving. The theme is the need
for man to praise God, so that he may regain the heaven
which was lost in disobedience and so that, God willing,
he may not suffer the punishments of the damned.

The theme of *Genesis* A is developed in an unusual
manner, a manner which cannot be understood without
reference to the principles of Christian literature that
were enunciated in the *De doctrina*. Although the poet
does not venture to leave his divinely inspired model,

the Bible, he does understand that his poem should be more than mere paraphrase or translation. He intends to enlighten and enkindle the minds of his audience to perceive the traditional doctrinal meaning underlying Genesis. But he understands that he is not himself a theologian and exegete. His poem must differ from commentary; and the difference will lie in his shaping—through modification and omission, but chiefly through amplification of thematic material—his biblical subject according to the demands of the underlying contrast between the two ways of life. But even in his handling of the Genesis material he follows the example of Moses, who, as Honorius of Autun says, was "willing in every way to adapt his material" so as to enforce the underlying truth of his history.[94]

The preceding long and detailed examination of the structure and plan of *Genesis* A is not intended to argue the suitability of the poem to modern tastes in poetry. Because the poem relies on a body of thought that has largely disappeared from the foreground of modern consciousness, it cannot act upon most modern readers in the way the poet intended. Yet, for the purpose of historical judgment—by which is meant a sympathetic, knowledgeable judgment—the analysis should provide a basis for understanding of intent; for analysis has shown that the poem is constructed according to the basic principles of the Christian theory of literature. *Genesis* A is not complex and subtle in structure as compared with other examples of OE poetry, but the poet's attention to form is of a kind which clearly places him in the line of the Christian writers who, through the medium of Augustine, inherited classical care for the subtleties of style.

The poet writes in English. His poem is not a translation from the Latin in any strict sense. He is thinking in English terms, making full use of, "re-employing," the language of his pagan ancestors for Christian purposes with flexibility and subtlety of connotation. If the poet of *Genesis* A is not Caedmon, he has at least a close literary affinity with Caedmon. But, of greater importance than the externals of style, the analysis of the poem has shown in detail how the poet has grounded his work firmly on the Bible, more precisely, on the underlying, spiritual meaning of the Bible which the Fathers had explored, developed, and set forth. *Genesis* A has a theme wrested out of the very structure of Genesis, out of the patristic understanding of the basic prophetic meaning of the first book of the Bible. In this sense, *Genesis* A stands at the beginning of the great medieval literature that, with the symbolic meaning of the Bible always at the center of consciousness, was to extend the imagination beyond the structural limitations of biblical commentary in such works of culmination as the *Divine Comedy* and *Piers Plowman*.

A question clearly remains from this study of Caedmon and *Genesis* A. What is the relation of this poetry to the body of OE poetry? The answer to this question must await a detailed study of each OE poem to see how far the principles of the Christian theory illumine what is dark and clarify what is obscure. But since some presumptive judgment may rightly be expected, the final chapter will be concerned with a brief attempt to sketch the possibilities inherent in the approach to OE poetry through the Christian theory of literature.

1. See *Records,* I, xxiv-xxvii, and C. Kennedy, *The Caedmon Poems* (London, 1916), pp. xxiii-xxv.
2. Bede, *PL,* 91, 13-14.
3. E. Sievers, "Caedmon und Genesis," in *Britannica* (Leipzig, 1929), pp. 57-84.
4. *PL,* 50, 1287.
5. See below, nn. 42-50.
6. See the discussion of *Daniel* in Ch. VI.
7. The translation is not based on the emendation accepted in *Records,* I, 3: *dæl* to *dwæl.* I amend only *weard* (l. 22) to *wearð,* taking this as the verb, with the subject, *dæl engla.*
8. See Pseudo-Bede, *Quaestiones super Genesim, PL,* 93, 246: "'Tales namque creati sunt angeli, ut si velint, in beatitudinis luce persisterent; si autem nollent, etiam labi potuissent. Unde et Satan cum sequacibus legionibus cecidit, sed post ejus lapsum ita confirmati sunt angeli, qui persisterunt, ut cadere omnino non possint.
9. Since the OE text is readily available, no gain in ease of reference would be secured by placing the original in footnotes. Except where the original language is specifically at issue only the Modern English version will be given.
10. Crawford, *op. cit.,* pp. 19-20. The translation, which is printed in Crawford's edition, is by L'Isle.
11. De Bruyne, *op. cit.,* p. 132. The French translation of the lines aptly fits the critical judgment made.
12. *Quaestiones veteris et novi testamenti,* 106. Compare Avitus, who in his *Libelli de spiritalis historiae gestis,* ed. C. Chevalier (Lyon, 1890), I, ll. 27-29, speaks of the immediate blooming of the woods at God's command,

> Sic ubere verbi
> Frondescunt silvae; teneris radicibus
> Duravit vastos arbor parvo sub tempore ramos.

See also *Genesis* A, l. 1137.
13. See Grein, *Sprachshatz, s.v., wan,* with its basic meaning of *deficiens,* and the various combinative words with *wan. Sinnihte*

may mean either "eternal-night" or "sin-night." The latter is perhaps preferable for its figurative meaning. Either interpretation of the word must be considered as figurative. The night, which is outside of God, cannot be eternal since God alone is eternal. Nor can the darkness itself be sinful. A literal interpretation of the word would involve the poet in the heresy of Manicheism, against which Augustine wrote a commentary on Genesis. (See Bede, *Hexameron, PL,* 91, 14.)

14. See Bede, *Hexameron, PL,* 91, 15.
15. *Liber formularum spiritalis intelligentiae, PL,* 50, 741.
16. For details see below, nn. 29 and 30.
17. Bede, *Hexameron, PL,* 91. Bede is followed in this division by Rabanus in his *Commentaria in Genesim, PL,* 107. The frequent references in this chapter to Bede are not intended to suggest a source in the poem. Bede's commentaries are used merely because they are appropriate, convenient, and succinct.
18. Bede, *Pentateuch, PL,* 91, 215; Bede, *Hexameron, PL,* 91, 61-62; see Augustine, *De Genesi ad litteram,* XI, 54-60; Rabanus, *PL,* 107, 500-502.
19. See Grein, *Sprachshatz.*
20. For this meaning of *wiste* see *Andreas,* l. 388, "God þe wist gife, heofonlicne hlaf"; *willgebroðor* is unique, and without the biblical connotations of the word it has little but mechanical significance.
21. *De civitate Dei,* XV, i, 2.
22. *Glossa ordinaria, PL,* 113, 98. The *glossa* is, of course, not the work of Strabo; it was probably compiled in the twelfth century, but it represents a compilation of standard patristic commentary. The actual source of the particular passage quoted I have not found. Compare Bede, *Hexameron, PL,* 91, 63-64.
23. *De civitate Dei,* XV, 7(1).
24. *Ibid.,* 1-8.
25. Pseudo-Bede, *Quaestiones, PL,* 93, 255-256. See Bede's *Hexameron, PL,* 91, 73; Rabanus, *In Genesim, PL,* 107, 506-507.
26. *De civitate Dei,* XV, 5.
27. *Pentateuch,* 219. (Reference here and after only to column and not to volume.)
28. *Ibid.,* 218.
29. *Hexameron,* 76. (Reference here and after only to column and not to volume.)
30. *Ibid.,* 69-70.

31. *Pentateuch,* 220.
32. *Hexameron,* 77.
33. *Hexameron,* 76-77. It is of some interest that the son of Seth, Enos, means "Man." To have this name rightly, Bede explains, is, remembering human frailty, to call upon the name of the Lord daily. Thus Enos "figuratively represents the Christian people."
34. *Ibid.,* 81.
35. *Pentateuch,* 221.
36. *Ibid.,* 224. Bede, of course, follows the Vulgate reading, *Permanebit.*
37. God's grief is recorded in Gen. 6:6. Bede, *Hexameron,* 84, following Augustine, explains that God's grief is metaphorical, an example of the manner in which Scripture, "se coaptat humili intelligentiae tardiorum." See *Pentateuch,* 225, where Bede connects the continuance of men in sin with the Fall. The one hundred and twenty years are symbolically meaningful.
38. The building of Noah's ark and the building of Solomon's temple permitted extraordinary development of number symbolism.
39. *Hexameron,* 97: *"sed et unde* tribulationum frequenter Ecclesiam pulsantes, quanto vehementius omnia repleverunt, tanto altius eam ad quaerenda vitae alterius gaudia compulerunt."
40. Crawford, *op. cit.,* p. 103.
41. *Ibid.,* p. 24.
42. *Hexameron,* 97-98.
43. See *Records,* I, 177.
44. *Pentateuch,* 223.
45. The context implies that the corrupt reading of l. 1405, *edmonne,* must have some such meaning as "the renewed one," or the like. The prefixed *ed-,* representing the Latin *re-,* seems correct. R. Wülker's suggestion, adopted by Krapp, *edmodne,* would be most satisfactory.
46. *Hexameron,* 99.
47. *Pentateuch,* 223; *Hexameron,* 100-102, for more detailed commentary.
48. *Ibid.,* 223.
49. *Ibid.*
50. *Hexameron,* 117-118. See the *Alethias* of Claudius Victor, trans. O. J. Kuhnmuench, *Early Christian Latin Poets,* pp. 338-342.
51. *Ibid.,* 120-121, see the *De civitate Dei,* XVI, xi, I.
52. *Pentateuch,* 229; in this act, Nimrod showed himself a son of

the Devil, Bede explains, for the Devil said, "I will ascend above the height of the clouds, and I will be like the Most High."

53. *Hexameron*, 125. A possible ultimate source for shifting the verse is suggested by Augustine, who remarks on the verse, *Quaestiones in Genesim*, I, 20, "Et erat omnis terra labium unum: quomodo hoc potest intelligi, quando superius dictum est quod filii Noe, vel filiorum ejus distributi essent per terram secundum gentes, et secundum linguas suas, nisi per recapitulationem postea commemorat quod prius erat? Sed obscuritatem facit quod eo genere locutionis ista contexit, quasi narratio de iis quae postea facta sunt, consequatur."

54. *Pentateuch*, 229.

55. Cited in the *Glossa ordinaria*, *PL*, 113, 114.

56. In *Exodus*, 203, the Egyptians, enemies of the Jews, are described in the midst of the plague as *feond anmod*. Nebuchadnezzar is called (*Daniel*, 224) *anmod cyning*, as he orders the furnace to be heated for the children of the Lord. In the *Runic Poem* the term is applied to the wild ox, who fights with his horns. In *Elene* the word is applied to the Jews as they are questioned by Elene and prepare to reply (396), and as they prepare to repent (1118). In the *Andreas* the word is used to refer to the Myrmidonians (1565 and 1601) as they prepare for baptism. Grein distinguishes between *ānmōd* and *anmōd*, but the distinction, based on nonexistent differences in meaning, seems unrealistic.

57. *Hexameron*, 128.

58. See comment on l. 117 above.

59. Line 1718 has not been amended, as is usual. I read *demað* as passive. Amended or not, the meaning remains about the same. It seems to me best to violate "grammar" and not the text.

60. *De civitate Dei*, XVI, 12; Bede, *Hexameron*, 133.

61. *De civitate Dei*, XVI, 10.

62. *Ibid.*, XVI, 12.

63. *Hexameron*, 134.

64. *Ibid.*, 140. A clear explanation is given by Rabanus, *PL*, 107, 534: "Quaeritur utrum conveniet Abram tam sancto viro ut celerat Saram uxorem suam, et cur non magis poneret spem suam in Deo, ne occideretur a rege. Ostenditur enim isto facto ejus quod homo non debet tentare Dominum Deum suum, quando habet quod faciet ex rationabili consilio. Fecit enim quod potuit

pro vita sua. Quod autem non potuit, illi commisit in quo speravit, cui et pudicitiam conjugis commendavit."

65. Rabanus, *PL*, 107, 536: "Typice autem beatus Abram discordiam pastorum suorum ac pastorum Lot vitare cupiens, et ob hoc secessem ab invicem eligens, nos admonet ut nihil charitati et concordiae praeponamus, sed semper parati simus, sive per prospera, quod dextra significat, sive per adversa, quae per sinistram exprimitur, in pace et dilectione perseverare." See *Hexameron*, 143.

66. *Hexameron*, 143. The land of the Sodomites is, like the land of Shinar, symbolic of earthly riches. The inhabitants of Sodom are iniquitous because, "maxima Dei munera non ad fructum pietatis, sed ad incrementum vertere luxuriae." It is interesting, in view of the poet's preceding use of the color, that he characterizes the land of Sodom as green, *Grene eorðan*. This is again the greenness of the fading flower. (See above, n. 58.) Different interpretations of the meaning of Lot's dwelling in Sodom appear. See Rabanus and Bede's *Pentateuch*, for example.

67. *PL*, 107, 533.

68. *Hexameron*, 144. Bede arrived at this interpretation by indirection from the underlying meaning of a passage (Lev. 6:13) that speaks of the never-failing fire of sacrifice, although the verse discussed by Bede (13:15) makes no mention of altar or sacrifice. However, Abraham built an altar and sacrificed after the second promise (12:7), and after the third promise he built an altar (13:18). Abraham's actions, symbolically interpreted by the aid of related passages like Lev. 6:13, helped to explain the meaning of God's promise.

69. *Hexameron*, 144.

70. *Pentateuch*, 230.

71. *Ibid.*

72. *Hexameron*, 149.

73. *Pentateuch*, 233; see Rabanus, *PL*, 107, 539.

74. *Glossa ordinaria*, *PL*, 113, 120. See *Hexameron*, 149: "Erant quippe trecenti decem et octo, quo nimirum numero signum victoriosissimae crucis et nomen Salvatoris nostri Jesu Christi, per quem hoc in munimentum nostrae salutis consecratum est, designatur. Si quidem apud Graecos trecenti per litteram T notantur, quae in crucis figuram aptatur. Nam si apicem in medio recepisset, non figura crucis, sed ipsum jam signum crucis manifeste

cerneretur expressum. Decem vero et octo apud eos per I et H quae in nomine Jesu primae sunt litterae notantur." Thus the number of the little band symbolizes "nasciturum de suo semine eum qui per passionem crucis mundum a morte revocaret."

75. Isidore of Seville, *Quaestiones in Genesim, PL*, 83, 239: "Sed quid haec victoria Abrahae de quinque regibus indicabat, quos ille fidei pater mysterio superavit, nisi quod fides nostra, si confirmata sit in spiritu principali, totidem corporis nostri sensus verbo Dei subigat? Nam sicut ille de proximo in regibus victor, ita et fides nostra per animam victrix de exteriore homine triumphat." See *Glossa ordinaria, PL*, 113, 120; Rabanus, *PL*, 107, 539; Bede, *Pentateuch*, 233.

76. *Hexameron*, 150-154.

77. *Hexameron*, 149.

78. *Hexameron*, 154; see *Pentateuch*, 234.

79. *Hexameron*, 153-154.

80. *Pentateuch*, 237.

81. The word "mine" is perhaps to be translated as a noun, love; God's love is a godly gift. "Love" is also a natural and simple reading of the word in *Wanderer*, 27, and *Beowulf*, 169. The objection to this reading of *Wanderer*, 27, in *Records*, III, 288, as "not authenticated for Anglo-Saxon" would rule out a great number of words of single or infrequent occurrence in OE.

82. *Hexameron*, 163.

83. *Ibid.*, 175, also 177-178, and *Pentateuch*, 239.

84. See nn. 58 and 66 above.

85. *Hexameron*, 178.

86. *PL*, 92, 548.

87. *Records*, I, xxiv-xxv.

88. *Ibid.*, xxv.

89. *CSEL*, 23, 231. See De Labriolle, *op. cit.*, pp. 473-474.

90. See above pp. 109, 135-137.

91. *CSEL*, 16, 359. See De Labriolle, *op. cit.*, pp. 726-727. The *Cento* of Proba carries the Old Testament narrative only to the Flood. See also Avitus, *Libelli de spiritalis historiae, MGH*, VI, 2.

92. *PL*, 172, 253.

93. Crawford, *op. cit.*, p. 26.

94. *PL*, 172, 253.

Chapter VI

CONJECTURES

EXCEPT for the *Hymn,* we do not know what Caedmon or his imitators wrote, but Caedmon's *Hymn* and *Genesis* A are connected unmistakably in spirit and tradition. Conjecturally, the body of OE poetry may also be considered as linked to these Caedmonian poems in the same Christian tradition. Such conjecture may be verified only through an intensive study of the body of OE verse in the light of the background of biblical exegesis. A study like this, as the analysis of *Genesis* A has shown, would have to be extremely detailed and would go beyond the modest scope of this book. A generalized survey, however, without any pretension to completeness or to detailed demonstration may have some usefulness in providing a series of working hypotheses. A start may be made by considering briefly the remaining three poems of the Caedmonian MS.

The second poem in the manuscript, the *Exodus,* must be understood, it seems to me, in the light of certain exegetical concepts developed by the Fathers in their commentaries on the portion of the Old Testament "paraphrased" in the English poem. Indeed, failure to take this principle into account has resulted in a presumption by scholars of difficulties in the text of *Exodus*. Attempts to resolve these often unreal difficulties have piled confusion upon fundamental misunderstanding. Nevertheless, J. W. Bright a considerable number of years ago made a beginning toward restoring order out of confusion by relating the poem to the liturgy for Holy Saturday.[1] Unfortunately, Bright contented himself with the evidence of modern liturgical practice. Moreover, many of the liturgical details were not to be found in the poem or were clearly out of line with it. The primary difficulty rested, of course, not so much with Bright's use of modern liturgy, which probably echoes old practice with sufficient accuracy, but in his failure to use scriptural commentary directly; for such commentary provides the conceptual source both of the liturgy and of the poem. The striking resemblances that Bright noted between liturgy and poem testify not to one as source of the other, but to a common source, biblical exegesis, for both.

Specifically, *Exodus* deals with the symbolic meanings of the biblical story of the Flight from Egypt and the Crossing of the Red Sea. The episode was of great importance in the prophetic symbolism of Christian interpretation of the Old Testament, for the Flight was taken to symbolize the escape from the world through Christ. The afflictions visited upon the Egyptians, their

218

drowning in the Red Sea, and, on the other hand, the Crossing by the Chosen, were all considered to have a significance connected with the drama of salvation. Such meanings are reflected in the following verses from the Latin *De cruce,* sometimes attributed to Erigena:

> Symbolically Moses is Christ, king and priest,
> who freed us when Egypt was subdued.
> He himself first submitted to death, and
> destroying death,
> leaped forth into life: having received the staff
> he rules.
> Why, Pharaoh, do you follow the people? Flee
> the engulfing depths!
> The black water of the eternal prison encompasses
> you.
> While we seek the middle road of virtue, above
> stand the domes of false-seeming and evil,
> which, mastering, the soul gains the joyful sands
> and sees, from afar, sins swallowed under the shore:
> then *alleluia* the soul sings, rejoicing and greatly
> triumphing,
> magnifies then with praises the mysteries of God.[2]

The symbolic meanings are inextricably connected with the biblical events themselves. When the poet speaks of Egypt, he clearly means the world *or* hell, from both of which Christ freed mankind. Conversely, when he speaks of the soul seeking the middle road of virtue above which the domes of evil tower, he is describing, on the historical level, the Crossing of the Red Sea. The Pharaoh represents the Devil. The waters represent sins or the love of the world in which the Egyptians, world-lings, drown. The deep into which they are hurled by the waters is hell; the joyful shore, reached by the paths of virtue, is heaven, where the rejoicing soul sings in praise of God.

The same symbolic meanings are celebrated in the OE *Exodus,* with great detail and in the epic manner of OE heroic poetry; that is, the poet of *Exodus* employs the manner of the Caedmonian poet in celebrating the victory of Abraham. Although *Exodus* is like *Genesis* A in following the biblical narrative of the Flight from Egypt, except for thematic alteration, addition, or transposition, the poet allows himself greater freedom in his thematic treatment of the biblical text than did the poet of *Genesis* A. *Exodus* is, in general, a more difficult poem than the other. The difficulties, however, are for the most part difficulties in symbolic interpretation, and they may be resolved by a close study of exegetical sources. Such a study would go beyond the limits of this chapter, but a brief glance at a few passages in the poem may be helpful in suggesting that the generalization may be supported from the text. The opening lines of *Exodus* suggest themselves as apparently thematic in intention:

> Hwæt! We feor and neah   gefrigen habað
> ofer middangeard   Moyses domas
> wræclico wordriht   wera cneorissum—
> in uprodor   eadigra gehwam
> æfter bealusiðe   bote lifes
> lifigendra gehwam   langsumne ræd—
> hæleðum secgan.   Gehyre se ðe wille!

Lo! Far and near we have heard/ over middle-earth the judgments of Moses/ the pilgrim law among the tribes of men—

in heaven to each of the blessed/ after the time of evil a
remedy for life;/ for each of the living an enduring counsel—/
told among men. Let him heed who will!

The epic formula with which the poem begins indicates
that the symbolic subject of *Exodus* is the law of Moses,
that is, the ten commandments. These are man's guide
in his Crossing through the towering temptations to the
joyful sands. Moreover, Moses not only represents the
old law, but prophetically symbolizes Christ, king, and
priest, and thus represents the new law as well. The
judgments of Moses are identified succinctly as a
wræclico wordriht, "pilgrim law," for his is the law of
the pilgrim seed of Seth, which leaves behind the king-
dom of this world, Egypt, to set forth on the Crossing.[3]
This law is heard when it is said (*secgan*) "among" or
"for" or "to" the tribes of men (*wera cneorissum*) and
men (*hæleðum*). But the concluding phrase, *hæleðum
secgan*, is suspended by the introduction of an emphatic
parenthesis. The parenthesis, in effect, defines the extent
of jurisdiction of the symbolic Mosaic law: it has been
efficacious for those who have already gained the joyful
sands, as the remedy for life, *bote lifes*, which has
brought them safe after the *bealusið*, the "time" or the
"journey" of sorrow, that is, bodily life and death. For
each man living, *lifigendra gehwam*, the law is an en-
during counsel, *langsumne ræd*, the consequences of
which, whether good or evil, are eternal. Let him heed
who will, "Gehyre se ðe wille!" The admonition indicates
that the poem will be concerned in its moral significance

221

with portraying the alternatives of obedience or disobedience to the law.

The punishment for disobedience is symbolically suggested in the lines from the poem which tell of the greatness of the day when the Hebrews left both Egypt and the Egyptians desolated (46-53):

> The temples in hell—heaven came there—
> the idols fell. The day was illustrious
> over middle-earth when the troop went forth.
> So this earthly prison bore for many years
> the perverse Egyptian folk
> because they thought, in the space of their days, to keep,
> if God had permitted them, the kinsmen of Moses
> from the long desire of the dear journey.

God declared to Moses (Exod. 12:12), "I will pass through the land of Egypt this night . . . and against all the gods of Egypt I will exact judgment." Heaven came on the night of the Passover to destroy the gods of this earth. Prophetically the acts symbolize the Resurrection, the Harrowing of Hell and the Freeing of the Captives. On another level, these events symbolize the eternal destruction of those who in disobedience live for the world and the escape of those who in obedience desire the dear journey.

To illustrate further, we find the poet describing the Crossing, then abruptly introducing a reference to the Flood and to earlier biblical history. As we have seen, the Flood represents the drowning of the worldlings and the salvation of the pilgrims. By recalling the Flood (ll. 362 ff.) the poet is actually suggesting the under-

lying meaning of the Crossing. Finally, the poem ends
with the song of rejoicing of the saved (Exod. 15:1-19)
and the dancing of Miriam and the Hebrew women
(Exod. 15:20-21). This last event is introduced allusively
in the poem (580-581):

> þa wæs eðfynde   Afrisc meowle
> on geofones staðe   golde geweorðod.

Then was it easy to find African maidens,/ adorned with gold,
on the stream's shore.

The much-debated term "African maidens" is probably
employed by the poet because of the African maiden of
the Song of Songs, traditionally a symbol of the bride
of Christ. As in the Latin *Exodus* poem, Miriam and the
Hebrew women, singing and dancing in praise, represent
the brides of Christ, that is, the souls of the blessed who
have gained the happy sands. Thus, the poem ends with
the theme of salvation and, in the last lines of the poem,
with the contrasting theme of damnation,

> Werigend lagon
> on deaðstede   drihtfolca mæst.

The protectors [of earthly treasure] lay/ in the place of death,
the mightiest of troops.

These illustrations from the *Exodus* of apparent thematic
intention should be sufficient to suggest the relevance of
exegetical symbolism to an understanding of the poem.
Exodus and the Caedmonian *Genesis* are apparently part
of one Christian tradition.

More lyrical in structure than *Genesis* or *Exodus,*

Doctrine and Poetry

Daniel, the third poem of the Junius MS, is similar to them in its apparent reliance on biblical symbolism. The theme of *Daniel* appears to be the familiar contrast between the ways of the righteous and the ways of the worldlings. *Daniel* begins:

Gefrægn ic Hebreos   eadge lifgean
in Hierusalem   goldhord dælan
cyningdom habban   swa him gecynde wæs
siððan þurh metodes mægen   on Moyses hand
wearð wig gifen   wigena mænieo
and hie of Egyptum   ut aforon
mægene micle.   Þæt wæs modig cyn.   [7]

þenden hie þy rice   rædan moston
burgum wealdon   wæs him beorht wela.
þenden þæt folc mid him   hiera fæder wære
healdan woldon   wæs him hyrde god
heofonrices weard   halig drihten
wuldres waldend.

                Se ðam werude geaf   [13]
mod and mihte   metod alwihta
þæt hie oft fela folca   feore gesceodon
heriges helmum   þara þe him hold ne wæs
oððæt hie wlenco anwod   æt winþege
deofoldædum   druncne geðohtas.   [18]

þa hie æcræftas   ane forleton
metodes mægenscipe   swa no man scyle
his gastas lufan   wið gode dælan.
þa geseah ic þe gedriht   in gedwolan hweorfan
Israhela cyn   unriht don
wommas wyrcean.   Þæt wæs weorc gode.   [24]

I heard that the Hebrews lived blessedly/ in Jerusalem, divided the store of gold,/ had kingdom as was theirs by nature's law/ since, through the might of God, into the hands of Moses/ was given the shrine of idols [*or,* skill at war], a multitude of warriors,/ and these from Egypt went forth/ through great might. That was a determined people./[7] While they through this power might take counsel/ they ruled over cities. Bright weal was to them/ while that folk with Him the faith of their fathers/ would keep, God was their Shepherd,/ the Ward of Heaven, the Holy Lord,/ Ruler of Glory. He it was who gave to that troop/[13] fortitude and strength, Almighty God/ that often they parted many folk from life,/ through the Protector of the Host, those who were not obedient to Him,/ until pride invaded them at the wine drinking/ through the devil's temptations, drunken thoughts./ [18] Then they abandoned their knowledge of the One Law,/ the brotherhood in God, though no man should/ separate the love of the soul from God./ Then I saw the band turn into heresy,/ the King of the Israelites do unrighteousness,/ work evil. That was a good work![24]

The poet takes great pains with the structural pattern of his verses. The phrase, "I heard" ("Gefrægn ic"), which introduces the first part of the thematic statement of contrast is balanced by the phrase "Geseah ic," which introduces the concluding statement. The two sentences that develop the theme of obedience are introduced by *þenden* (8 and 10), the two that develop the theme of disobedience are introduced by *þa* (19 and 22). Set off, "framed," by these parallel contrasting statements is the explanation of how those who were faithful fell into evil ways (13-18). Finally, the summarizing phrases of the initial and concluding passages are parallel in structure: "þæt wæs modig cyn," "þæt wæs weorc gode." But it is particularly in his Augustinian playing with words that the poet of *Daniel* shows himself most notably in the Christian tradition of poetry.

The parallel sentences last noted, for example, are balanced not only in structure, but in irony of phrasing. The fall into evil is clearly not a "good work." The meaning of *modig* in the first sentence has a similar ironic ambiguity, for *modig* has two directly opposite meanings, "proud" and "magnanimous." Thus the King of Babylon, an evil persecutor, is called *modig* (105). The distinction in meaning rests, of course, in the underlying bent of any individual greatness of heart. The same greatheartedness that in obedience to God led the Hebrews out of Egypt led the great King of the World to self-glorification and will lead the Hebrews back into bondage. While the Hebrews lived in Jerusalem, that is, as pilgrims toward heaven, they divided the treasure (*goldhord dælan*, 2), that is, the treasure of spiritual gold. When they abandoned the Faith of Abraham, their hearts turned to love of themselves, self-glorification, so that they separated themselves from God (*wið Gode dælan*, 21); they fell into heresy (*in gedwolan*, 22). The play on *goldhord dælan, wið Gode dælan, gedwolan*, is particularly remarkable in that it extends over more than twenty lines. The wordplay serves to enforce the thematic contrast and the explanation for the change from faith to faithlessness. Another play on the similar sounds of words occurs in line 5, *wig gifen, wigena*. This wordplay is perhaps intended to suggest a possible pun on the word *wig*, which means either "heathen shrine," "idol," or "battle" (that is, strength in battle). Through the *strength* God gave him, Moses overthrew the *idols* of the Egyptians. While the Hebrews lived according to nature, or

natural law (*gecynde,* 3), God's law on earth, they took
counsel (*rædan,* 8), lived by reason; then they wielded
(*weoldan*) cities in weal (*wela,* 9, with possible play on
wel don, did well). The wordplay of the opening lines re-
appears in extraordinary profusion throughout the poem.
Daniel would appear to belong to the same tradition of
poetry as *Genesis* A.

The final poem of the Junius MS, editorially called
Christ and Satan, unlike the other poems, is not based
on a single portion of the Bible. This difference, however,
is not decisive. The position of the Bible as the model
of true poetry does not imply, of course, that Christian
poetry must limit itself to paraphrasing or moralizing
of the Bible. As Augustine points out, although there is
only one truth, the one truth has many facets. Christian
poetry could be most varied in subject and manner, pro-
vided that it led to the truth. The substance of *Christ
and Satan,* moreover, is either biblical or derived from
the same hexameral tradition that supplied many of the
concepts found in poems already discussed. *Christ and
Satan* tells first of the Defeat of the Fallen Angels, then
of Christ's Harrowing of Hell, finally of the Temptation
of Christ by Satan. The alteration of biblical order in the
poem, the Temptation coming after the Harrowing, has
caused some scholars to dismember the poem, in spite
of the evidence that the compiler of the poem assumed
it to be one. To feel that something is wrong struc-
turally with *Christ and Satan* is to miss the theme of the
poem, which is clearly stated at the beginning. This
theme is the incommensurate might of God.

Doctrine and Poetry

The poet begins (1-18):

> It was manifest to mankind
> that *the Master had might and strength*
> when He fashioned the fields of earth.
> *Selfsame He set* the sun and the moon,
> the stars and the earth, the stream in the sea,
> the water and the sky, *through His wondrous might.*
> The deep expanse entirely encompasses He,
> *the Master in His might,* and all the middle-earth;
> He Godself may gaze through the sea,
> the deeps in heaven, the dear Son of God,
> and reckon He can the rain showers,
> singly each drop: the sum of all days
> *Selfsame He set through His soothfast might.*
> So the Creator through the Holy Spirit
> planned and set in six days
> the earthly regions, up in heaven,
> and the deep waters. *Who is it that knows*
> *the skill entirely except Eternal God?*

This introductory passage again illustrates the Caedmonian handling of creation, as revealing to man the power of God and His trinitarian nature. But attention may be given here only to the clarity of thematic statement achieved at the beginning of a poem that, by the evidence of these opening lines, should not be called *Christ and Satan,* but *The Might of God.* The theme suggested by this title is brought out in the most emphatic way possible in the structural repetition indicated by the italicized phrases. The Defeat of the Angels, the Harrowing, the Temptation of Christ, in varying ways illustrate this might. The theme itself is repeated throughout the poem. For example (32-33):

228

Conjectures

God ana wat
hu he þæt scyldige werud   forscrifen hefde.

God alone knows/ how He that guilty host had punished.

In the succeeding lines God's terrible triumph over Satan
is shown in dramatic detail. The narrative is interrupted
by an incremental thematic restatement, which begins
(193-201):

> Therefore must each man take thought
> that he offend not the Son of God.
> Let each regard as an example how the black devils
> through pride all perished.
> Let us choose as our delight, the Lord of Hosts
> on high, Eternal Joy, Ruler of Angels.
> *He made it known that He had strength,*
> *great might,* when he expelled that rout,
> captives from the high hall.

This restatement provides a moral application of the
theme. Another such restatement is made in lines which
also deal with the Defeat of Satan (282-300):

> Therefore should he think, whose heart is good,
> that he put aside evil thoughts,
> wicked infamies, each of the living.
> *Let us ever remember in mind the strength of God,*
> prepare for the green streets
> up with the angels where is Almighty God. . . .
> 　　　　　　　　*Let us proclaim that!*　　　　　[297]
> Let us announce on earth while we are living,
> *reveal with skills the secrets of God,*
> perceive spiritually.

Still another thematic restatement on the level of moral
application is found on the same subject of the Defeat
of Satan (348-352):

Doctrine and Poetry

There is none so wise or so strong,
nor of this so wise except God Himself
that may tell the light of heaven,
how the splendor there shines about
through might of God over that glorious brotherhood.

The section dealing with the Harrowing of Hell contains similar thematic restatements (582-584):

That is known to many
that *He alone* is of all creation
Creator and Ruler *through His strength of glory*.

A direct moral application to man's situation is made in the same section of the Harrowing (642-669):

Let us then consider in this world
that we the Saviour begin to praise,
eagerly through God's gift remember the glory of the soul,
how the blessed above there dwell,
themselves in harmony, the sons of the Saviour. . . .
So the Ward of Heaven with words they praise,   [659]
retainers about the Lord. There is much glory,
song at the throne. The King Himself is
the Lord of all in the eternal creation.
That is God Who for us death
endured, the Lord of Angels.
Likewise He fasted for forty days,
the Lord of Mankind through mercy's victory.
Then it chanced the accursed, who erewhile was cast out
of heaven, dove into hell,
when he tempted the King of all Creation.

The thematic statement, with its clear moral application to man, leads transitionally to the third and final section, the Temptation. The thematic transition suggests the

230

poet's principle of formal construction, with its apparent inconsistency in placing the Temptation after the Harrowing. The Temptation, no less than the Defeat of the Angels and the Harrowing, reveals the might of God, but more particularly, with relation to man, it represents the supreme example of how man, though burdened by the flesh, should imitate God. The Temptation is climactic, not historically, but tropologically (morally), and thus it serves admirably as the climax of the three symbolic events that reveal God's might and define man's duty. The Temptation ends the poem because it is tropologically the supreme drama in God's defeat of Satan. For it was Christ the man whom Satan tempted, and in repelling the Temptation Christ showed how mankind should also repel temptation. *Christ and Satan* begins with the theme of the power and might of God; paradoxically, in the humility of Christ's assumption of humanity He triumphs most profoundly. The structural unity of *Christ and Satan*, like that of the *Genesis* A, rests on the understanding of the underlying meaning of biblical narrative.

We could proceed, as we have with the Junius MS, through the body of OE poetry, that is, until we came to the poems of pagan subject, which seem, thus, to be apart from the Christian-Caedmonian influence. Some of the finest OE lyrics fall in this class, and so also does the *Beowulf*. Although it is impossible to give any detailed consideration of the *Beowulf* here, some tentative conjectures may be made, since the groundwork for a thoroughgoing Christian interpretation has already been laid. Klaeber has shown in minute detail that the so-called "Christian elements" are an indigenous part of the *Beowulf;* they may not be neatly divided from the "pagan elements." [4] Tolkien, with finality, has exposed the folly of the literal-minded approach to the *Beowulf,* with its air of entering a curio shop to look at the quaint, the simple, the naïve. He showed that the monsters in *Beowulf* have symbolic meaning, that the poem is a significant human document. [5] Kemp Malone has demonstrated the unity of narrative in the work. [6]

There remains, however, the task of viewing the *Beowulf* directly in the light of the Augustinian-Caedmonian tradition. The poem itself contains many obvious leads. Grendel is connected with Cain, for example, and the scop in Heorot sings a song of Genesis, which arouses the ancient, tainted blood of Grendel to fury. As Tolkien in a general way has shown that the monsters in *Beowulf* have human meaning, we may, in specific Christian terms, show what that meaning was likely to be. For example, Isidore, in the *Etymologiae,* has some significant remarks about the meaning of portents, prodigies, monsters. What binds these words together for Isidore is that each, apparently contrary to nature, is a sign sent by God to warn or admonish. [7] Grendel and the dragon might well have had such a definite symbolic force for the Christian audience. Grendel, the monster, seems, in fact, to serve as a warning, a portent to the Danes of impending disaster, if it is not fortuitous that Grendel makes his appearance at Heorot at a time when discord is beginning to threaten the kingdom. This discord is suggested by hint and warning throughout the narrative. Beowulf's own account of the state of Denmark is filled with a sense of doom. In turn the long and bitter struggle between the Geats and the Swedes is not ended with the death of Beowulf. The sense of doom hangs heavily over the last portion of the narrative and is intensified in Wiglaf's lament. The dragon is again portentous in his appearance.

Until *Beowulf* is systematically studied from the tentative assumption that the poet, in accord with Christian theory, was consciously restoring pagan truth to its Master, the place of the epic in the Christian tradition cannot be stated with any finality; that is, a systematic test should be made of the assumption that the *Beowulf* was written by a learned Christian, one for whom the Bible, with its vast accretion of symbolic meanings, was central in the interpretation of all events, even those of the mythical pagan past of his race. There is more than a little to suggest that such study will reveal the epic to be in the direct line of Christian tradition.

The two famous poems from the Exeter Book, the *Wanderer* and the *Seafarer,* because they are brief, may more readily than the *Beowulf* be shown to belong to the tradition of Christian poetry. The structural and thematic unity of the *Wanderer* as a Christian poem seems demonstrable from the study of the poem itself. Some time ago the present writer made a detailed attempt to show that the poem was structurally unified, but without any attempt to relate the structure to a tradition.[8] By reference to some primary truths of Christian thought Professor Lumiansky has advanced further in the same direction. He makes abundantly clear the poet's essential Christian bias.[9] Even more clearly, Professor D. W. Robertson, Jr., in a paper as yet unpublished, has taken the necessary steps to show that the *Wanderer* employs very conventional biblical symbolism. At the very center of the poem is the image of wandering, symbolic of life on this earth. The exile is, in Christian symbolism, man on earth, seeking his true home and his true king. The so-called gnomic sections in the poem also have direct parallels in Christian writing. The poet's adjuration, for example, that a man be not hasty in act or speech reflects Christian moral injunction as much as it does the behavior pattern of Germanic heroic paganism, which has been reconstructed largely through the instrumentality of Christian texts. Indeed, no heroic writings of Germanic paganism actually survive, so that the *only* moral tradition that we can postulate historically for the *Wanderer* is the Christian tradition.

With a knowledge of the Christian principles of composition in mind, it is not difficult to see that the *Wanderer* is an inevitable extension of what we have found in *Genesis* A. The poet leaves the strict confines of biblical story to imagine the symbolic figure of the exile. He pictures him bereaved, alone, without friends, searching for a lord. Professor Robertson sees in this picture only the symbol of the Christian lost in the world, yearning for his heavenly home. He finds the postulate of pagan background unessential, even misleading. Though I disagree with Professor Robertson's literary judgment here and insist that the poet is picturing the heroic, pagan figure of the exile, the Christian commentary loses none of its force. True grief for the Christian is caused only by separation from God. In my view, the exile in the *Wanderer* grieves precisely because he yearns for the consolations of an earthly lord, because his mind is darkened by his earthly sorrows. Against such a picture, the Christian audience had the steady vision of the good man, like Abraham, who kept bright his faith in God, whose mind could never be darkened by sorrow because his heart was not set on the things of this world. Moreover, against the picture of the exile is set, in my opinion, the picture of a wise man, who ponders apart, away from the world, and who sees that all the world decays, that there is nothing steadfast upon which man may count—except, as the poem concludes, the hope that he may gain the eternal home in heaven.

What has been said of the *Wanderer* holds with equal force for the *Seafarer*. O. S. Anderson, by an analysis of the poem itself, has come to the conclusion that it is to be interpreted as symbolizing the journey in life toward death.[10] Anderson's study, which claims simply to make better sense of the poem than any approach by way of reconstructed heroic material, may be supported and reinforced in detail from biblical commentary and Christian commonplace. The symbols in the poem spring from the conventions of Christian thought, the substance of homily and tract. To show that the *Seafarer* is a logical development of Christian biblical poetry it is necessary merely to show in detail the actual significance of the symbols employed.

The theme postulated for the *Wanderer* and the *Seafarer* is overtly echoed in the consolatory lyric, *Deor:*

> He who sits sorrowful, deprived of joys,
> grows dark in his mind: he thinks to himself
> that the portion of sorrows may be endless.
> Yet may he think that in this world
> wise God often varies:
> to many an earl He shows grace,
> true glory; to others a portion of woe.

The advice is familiar: The Lord giveth and the Lord taketh away. Man must think not of his earthly but of his heavenly lot. Even *Widsith,* with its long mnemonic catalogue of heroic names, leads to a Christian commentary on what Widsith, the far-traveler, has seen in voyage through the world:

> So I that ever found on the journey
> that he is most beloved among the dwellers on earth
> to whom God gives rule over men
> to hold while he here lives.

The poem concludes:

> lof se gewyrce
> hafað under heofonum heahfæstne dom.

He who earns praise/ has under heaven a glory set on high.

The lives of great men all remind us—the lines echo in meaning Caedmon's *Hymn.*

Finally, there is the poem that marks the end of traditional OE verse, the *Battle of Maldon.* Much attention has been paid to the heroic quality of this poem, and it has been called more perfectly heroic in spirit than anything except a few portions of the *Iliad*. Yet Brythnoth, the hero, was historically celebrated for his piety and for his benefactions to English monasteries, and one wonders how "purely heroic" is Brythnoth's challenge to the Vikings (93-95):

> Now room has been made for you: come quickly to us,
> men to battle. God alone knows
> who will possess the place of slaughter.

Like Brythnoth, Abraham facing battle against unbelievers,

> said that to him the Holy
> Eternal Lord easily might
> at the spear-violence grant victory.   [*Genesis* 2057-2059]

Would not Abraham, the warrior, have come more readily to the mind of Brythnoth's audience than a distant, suppositious hero of the pagan past. Moreover, if Brythnoth is not thought of as being essentially Christian, as embodying the highest principles of Christian conduct in the active life, then the contrast between him and the Viking wolves is lost. Concentration on the heroic elements in *Maldon* will tend to lessen the effectiveness of Brythnoth's saintly death. He dies like a Christian martyr, not like the "heroic" Viking wolves who slew him, and it is the spirit of his dying words, which most completely illumines the entire poem, that makes Brythnoth worthy of the veneration English monks gave him for centuries (173-180):

I thank Thee, Ruler of Men,
for all the joys which I had on earth:
Now I have, merciful Lord, the greatest need
that Thou grant my spirit grace
that my soul to Thee may come
into Thy power, Lord of Angels,
pass with peace. I beseech Thee
that the fiends of hell may not harm it.

This dying speech is far from the "purely heroic." There is no lament over past glory, no sorrow over defeat. There is simply single-minded, saintly praise of God by a devout Christian who has served his time on earth and begs God now to receive him in his heavenly home. The speech is inappropriate to a dying Hector or a dying Siegfried. It is appropriate to a Christian martyr. The spirit of Brythnoth's dying speech in this last of the great OE poems reflects the beginnings of that poetry. It has the same devout and all-consuming faith which animates the poetry of Caedmon.

These remarks on the relation of the body of OE poetry to Caedmon's *Hymn* and to the Caedmonian *Genesis* are but remarks, tentative and hypothetical. They are intended not as judgments, but rather as indications of a possible direction for the study of OE poetry. I have tried to show that Caedmonian poetry is in the direct line of the tradition formulated for the Middle Ages by Augustine. It is a tradition which has its roots in the culture of the classical world but which is profoundly modified by Christianity, with its allegorical turn of thought arising from the belief that the techniques of biblical interpretation are capable of penetrating to the word of God in so far as God permitted. The Christian theory of poetry was clear and definite; it was subscribed to by all Christians. The practice of Latin Christian poetry was in accord with the theory. Caedmon's English poetry was also in accord with the theory. Since the body of OE poetry is Christian, it should be studied, whatever its subject, from the point of view of basic Christian theory and practice. It may well be that when the relation of such poetry to biblical symbolism has been explored fully it will be possible to see clearly the place of OE poetry in relation not only to Latin Christian poetry, but to late medieval poetry as well. It may become possible to speak of one great, universal tradition of Christian poetry, written by men who sought rather to drink from the well of living water than from the springs of Helicon.

1. "The relation of the Caedmonian Exodus to the Liturgy," *MLN,* XXVII (1912), 97-103.
2. A. Mai, *Classicorum auctorum e Vaticanis,* V (Rome, 1833), 430-431:

   > Mysticus est Moyses Christus, rex atque sacerdos,
   > Qui nos Aegypto liberat edomita.
   > Ipse subit mortem primus, mortemque resolvens
   > Prosilet in vitam: Virga recepta regit.
   > Quid Pharao sequeris populam? fuge mersus in ima:
   > Carceris aeterni te tegit atra palus.
   > Nos virtutis iter medium dum carpimus, alte
   > Instant phantasiae nequitiaeque tholi.
   > Quas vincens animus laeta potitur haerena,
   > Et peccata procul mersa sub acta videt.
   > Tunc *Alleluia* canit gaudens multumque triumphans,
   > Laudibus amplificat tunc paradoca Dei.

3. *Wræclico* may also mean "bitter," "wondrous," and "exile"; these meanings add connotational depth to the word as it is used in the poem; the law given to the exiles from Paradise is bitter to the Babylonians, wondrous to the true pilgrim.
4. "Die Christlichen elemente in Beowulf," *Anglia* XXXV (1911), 111-156, 249-270, 453-482; XXXVI (1912), 169-199.
5. J. R. R. Tolkien, *Beowulf: The Monsters and the Critics* (London, 1938).
6. Kemp Malone, "Beowulf," *English Studies,* XXIX (1948), 162-172.
7. "De portentis," in *Etymologiae,* ed. Lindsay, XI, iii.
8. *JEGP,* XLII (1939), 515-538.
9. R. M. Lumiansky, "The Dramatic Structure of the Old English Wanderer," *Neophilogus,* XXXIV (1950), 104-112. Between this time and the final preparation of this book for the press (1956), much interesting work has been done on the elegies by D. Whitelock, S. B. Greenfield, and—most recently and most excellently— by E. G. Stanley in *Anglia* LXXIII (1956), 413-466; in this latter article I find some happy confirmations of my conjectures.
10. *"The Seafarer," an Interpretation* (Kungl. Humanistiska Vetenskapssamfundets i Lund Arsberattekse, 1937).

Index

Index

diction, 66, 67, 117, 118, 121, 122; *see* epithets; vocabulary
Dido, 5
difficulty, 10-12, 18, 22, 24, 30, 32, 50, 51, 55, 220; *see* obscurity
Dionysius, 62
Divider, 146
Dobbie, E., 95
Doctor, Good, 136
doctrine, Christian, 48, 52, 69, 79, 93, 104, 197; *see* sentence; truth; dogma
dogma, 23, 24, 65; *see* doctrine, Christian; sentence; truth
Donatus, 39, 41-43, 46, 59
dove, 66, 175
dragon, 232, 233
dress, 35-37
drowning, 219, 222
Duemmler, E., 95
Duke, 66, 118

earth, 108, 113, 115, 117, 120, 141, 144, 150, 153, 160, 161, 183, 184, 192, 194, 199, 222; adornment of the, 115, 116
east, 146, 183-185, 190
Egypt, 4, 67, 189, 195, 214, 219, 221, 222, 225, 226; *see* Flight from
Ehwald, R., 95, 96, 130
Elene, 214
Ellis, R., 95
eloquence, 5-9, 13, 16, 29, 30, 36, 37, 48, 51, 52; *see* poetry
English, 55, 67-69, 73-75, 78, 80, 86, 88, 89, 93, 94, 99, 121, 209
enjoyment; *see* use and enjoyment
enigmatic, 30, 32, 44, 55, 56, 72, 74, 79, 124; *see* obscurity
Enoch, 165, 166
Enos, 213
epithets, 65, 66, 69, 70, 109, 116, 118-121, 146, 147, 198; *see* diction
Erigena, John Scotus, 46, 52-55, 62, 130, 219; *De cruce,* attributed to, 219, 220, 223
eternity (eternal), 113-117, 144-146, 162, 175, 235
etymology, 33, 34, 76
Eucherius of Lyons, 26, 28, 29, 57, 60, 66, 128
Eusebius (Hwætberht), 55; (historian), 127
Eustatius, 104, 128, 129
Eve, 82, 90, 91, 98, 141, 147, 149-151, 154-156, 158, 159, 163, 176

evil, 6, 17, 23, 79, 92, 139, 149, 152, 156, 158, 168, 184
exegesis (exegetical), 4, 12, 15, 21, 29, 38, 43, 84, 89, 113, 123, 124, 148, 150, 153, 155, 159, 164, 165, 167, 168, 174, 175, 190, 208, 217, 218, 220, 223; *see* commentary (commentator), biblical
exercise, mental or intellectual, 9, 16, 22, 24, 29, 34, 37, 42, 53-56, 73, 75, 89, 94, 124; *see* pleasure, aesthetic; obscurity, scriptural and literary
exile, 92, 149, 151, 234, 235
Exodus, 131, 214, 217, 218, 220-223; theme of, 220-223
expulsion from Paradise, 149-152, 158, 159; *see* exile

fables, 11, 14, 17, 24, 30, 33, 118; *see* fiction; lies
fact, 43, 45, 51, 54, 55, 66, 77; writer of, 50
Faith, 7, 13, 19, 36, 43, 48, 54, 65, 103, 109, 172, 182, 188, 189, 192, 194-197, 216, 225
Fall, 82-84, 135, 137, 152, 153, 162, 168, 174, 176, 226; *see* damnation
Fate and Fortune, 72, 76
fiction, 4, 17, 30, 31, 51, 53, 54, 69-71, 80; *see* fable; lies
field, flowery, 80, 82, 85, 88, 89
fifteen, 172
figurative, 11, 14, 18, 19, 21-24, 31, 42, 49, 51, 53, 55, 141, 159, 164, 181, 192, 234
figure of speech, 10, 14-16, 35, 36, 38, 42, 47, 54, 147, 159, 169
Five Boroughs, 154
five kings, 195-197, 216
fleshly robes, 8, 13, 16; *see* dress; literal
Flight from Egypt, 5, 218, 220
Flood, 135, 136, 158, 162, 166, 168, 170-174, 176, 178, 222; *see* waters
flower, 44, 84-86, 88
form, 8, 16, 22, 37, 42, 106, 107; *see* order; structure
fountain, 71, 88, 93; *see* well
four kings, 195-197
fruit, 83, 158, 159, 191
Fulgentius, 30, 67, 95

garden, 82, 83, 91, 93, 145, 147, 149, 187; *see* field, flowery; Paradise
gate, guarding of, 150-152, 162, 176

Index

Index

Japheth, 177-180; generation of, 178, 181
Jenkinson, F., 63
Jerome, St., 51, 52, 60, 62, 127
Jerusalem, 4, 41, 45, 121, 156, 160, 161, 164, 175, 177, 182, 187, 188, 203, 224, 226
Jesse, 44
Josephus, 203
journey, 5, 7, 120, 173, 183, 222, 235; *see* pilgrimage
Jones, C., 57
Jubal, 161
Junius MS, 131, 204, 224, 227, 231
Junius Philargyrius Grammaticus, 57
Jupiter, 71

Kane, G., 127
Keil, H., 59
Kennedy, C., 211
King, 66, 70, 118-121, 134, 146, 219, 221, 225, 226, 234
Klaeber, F., 232
Krapp, G., 95, 213
Kuhnmuench, O., 95, 127, 128, 213

Labriolle, de, P., 19, 25, 26, 45, 59, 60, 127, 128, 216
Lactantius, *Phoenix* attributed to, 67
Laistner, M., 95, 96, 128
Lamech, 148, 161-164, 166
language(s) (tongue), 19, 20, 23, 39, 65, 68, 70, 72, 103, 105, 110, 121, 182, 183, 185, 187
Latin, 65, 67-69, 76, 78, 83, 88, 94, 99, 104, 123, 127, 128, 209
law, 220, 221, 224-227
learning, 3-5, 7, 8, 22, 49, 88, 104
leaves, 83, 85, 86, 92, 158, 160
Legouis, E., 142, 143
Lehmann, P., 60
Leon, P. and M., 26
letter, 8, 14, 16-18, 20, 23, 37, 46, 47, 52, 55, 71, 125, 143; *see* literal
letters, 3-5, 7, 20, 29, 33, 34, 52; *see* literature
liberal arts, 22, 33, 47, 50; *see* program, Augustine's
Licentius, 12, 17
lies (lying), 4, 15, 17, 117; *see* fables; fictions
light, 145, 146, 183, 184
Lindsay, W., 57, 59, 96, 98, 127
lion, 66
literal, 18-20, 22, 23, 37, 42, 51, 70; *see* letter; fleshly robes

literal meaning, 37, 42, 49
literature, 5, 8, 10, 13, 17, 19, 22, 30, 36, 52; purpose of, 18, 46, 55; Augustinian theory of, 18, 23, 24, 29, 32, 36-38, 46, 55, 56, 65, 124, 125, 132, 133, 207, 208, 210, 233; *see* letters; poetics; theory, aesthetic
liturgy, 64, 128, 142, 218
Löhe, H., 96
lorica, 74-77; *see* breastplate; cuirass
Lot, 186-189, 191, 195, 196, 199, 202, 215; wife of, 203, 204
Lot, F., 26
love; *see* charity
Lucifer, 118, 141, 158, 164, 178, 219; *see* Satan
Lumiansky, R., 234, 240

Maeldubh, 69
Magoun, F., 130
Mai, A., 63, 240
Malone, K., 232, 240
man, a lonely; *see* aloneness
Manitius, M., 63, 95, 96
Marrou, H-I, 11, 19, 25-27, 57, 59, 73, 96
Mary, 44
Master, 6
meaning, underlying or biblical, 8, 9-11, 13, 14, 16, 20, 22-24, 29, 31, 33-35, 37, 38, 42, 44, 46, 47, 50, 54, 62, 66, 74, 81, 83, 87, 89, 90, 94, 102, 104, 107, 114, 116, 124, 125, 134, 135, 143, 146, 150, 157, 161, 162, 171, 175, 176, 183, 188, 192, 193, 206, 208, 209, 231; *see* allegory; sentence; symbol
Melchisedech, 198, 199
memory, 123
Mercury, 5
metrics, 51, 68, 73
middle-earth, 101, 108, 115, 116, 118, 120
Might of God, 101, 108, 109, 111, 227, 228, 231
Miller, T., 127
miracle, 101-103, 122, 196
Miriam, 223
model, Bible as, 5, 9, 23, 31, 33, 36, 38, 54, 60, 122, 227; *see* Bible, pre-eminence of
Mohrmann, C., 59
Moricca, U., 26, 95, 96
Moses, 73, 104-106, 206, 208, 219-221, 224

245

Index

mount, 71, 120, 172, 174
Muses, 70
music, 21
mustard seed, 54, 55
myth, 30, 66, 67, 70-72, 120, 233

nakedness, 176, 178
native land, 7, 75, 152; *see* heaven; home; *patria*
natural history, 21, 49
Neptune, 13-15
night, 144, 145
Nimrod, 178-183, 187, 213
Noah, 136, 165, 169-176, 178
numbers, 21, 107, 162

obscurity, scriptural and literary, 9, 11, 12, 18, 20, 22, 24, 29, 32, 34, 35, 41, 42, 49, 50, 53, 54-56, 60; *see* ambiguity; difficulty; enigmatic
Old English; *see* English
Olympus, 67, 69-71, 120, 136
one hundred and twenty years, 166, 168, 213
Orientius, *Explanatio nominum domini* attributed to, 66
ord (beginning), 100, 118, 119

parable, 14, 37, 41, 54, 70
Paradise, 85, 89, 90, 91, 150, 158, 184; *see* garden
Paré, G., 27
Passion, Christ's, 164
patria, 192, 193; *see* home; native land
Patrick, St., *Lorica* of, 77
Paul, St., 7, 17, 18, 43, 54, 198
peace, 165, 182
pearl, 15, 54, 81; Pearl, 66
penance; *see* repentance
Peter, St., 198
Pharaoh, 219
pigs, 14; *see* swine
pilgrim (pilgrimage), 6, 7, 79, 160, 161, 174, 175, 181, 194, 220-222, 226; *see* journey
pillar of salt, 203
Pitman, J., 96
Phoebus Apollo, 67, 70, 71
Phoenix, 67, 70
Plato, 3
pleasure, aesthetic or literary, 9, 11, 16, 17, 23, 24, 29, 31, 33, 34, 50, 52, 53, 55, 62; *see* beauty, poetic; obscurity, scriptural and literal

Plummer, C., 96, 127
poem, 5, 12, 51, 56, 78, 87, 99, 105
poet, 3, 11, 12, 16, 50, 51, 54, 74, 86, 88-90, 93, 121, 126, 205; Christian, 12, 13, 16, 30, 31, 45, 65, 67, 81, 84, 93, 94; pagan, 51, 52, 66
poetics (poetic theory), 9, 30, 34, 49, 67, 75, 99, 157, 234, 239; *see* literature, theory of; theory, aesthetic
poetry, 4, 12, 16, 19, 51, 55, 64, 65, 72, 83, 95, 102, 118, 123, 124, 227; Christian Latin, 64, 67, 68, 73, 81, 86, 87, 94, 117, 118, 239; Christian English, 68, 73, 86, 87, 94, 99, 101, 103, 117, 153, 217, 239; justification for, 69, 94, 99, 122, 132; pagan Latin, 51, 71; vernacular, 67, 68, 74, 105, 121
possession, 155, 156, 183, 184
praise, theme of, 72, 100, 101, 108, 109, 111, 112, 115-117, 134, 135, 137, 138, 142, 144, 159, 176, 206, 238
Preface of the Mass, 108, 109, 123, 128, 134, 137
Prince, 66
principle, Augustinian; *see* literature, theory of
Proba, *Cento* of, 67, 216
Prodigal Son, 14, 15
program, Augustine's, 20, 22, 29, 69; *see* Augustine; liberal arts; training
promises, God's, 191-193, 200, 201, 204
Pseudo-Bede, 211, 212
psychomachia, 197
purification, 51-53; *see* exercise, intellectual
Pyramus and Thisbe, 12, 17

Rabanus, 28, 49-52, 61, 62, 192, 212, 214-216,
Raby, F., 58, 95
Rand, E., 25, 26, 57, 59, 61, 63, 127
raven, 174, 175
Red Sea, Crossing of, 218, 219, 221-223
Redemption, 135, 137, 158, 159, 162-164, 166, 168, 174-176, 180, 188, 192, 197, 198, 200, 206; *see* Salvation
Régnier, A., 59
repentance, 80, 83, 84, 93

246

Index

Index

Citations from Scripture (*Vulgate*)